How China Grows

How China Grows

INVESTMENT, FINANCE, AND REFORM

James Riedel, Jing Jin, and Jian Gao

PRINCETON UNIVERSITY PRESS   PRINCETON AND OXFORD

Copyright © 2007 by Princeton University Press
Published by Princeton University Press, 41 William Street, Princeton,
New Jersey 08540
In the United Kingdom: Princeton University Press, 3 Market Place,
Woodstock, Oxfordshire OX20 1SY
All Rights Reserved

Library of Congress Cataloging-in-Publication Data

Riedel, James.
How China grows : investment, finance, and reform / James Riedel, Jing Jin,
and Jian Gao.
p. cm.
Includes bibliographical references and index.
ISBN-13: 978-0-691-12562-6 (cl : alk. paper)
ISBN-10: 0-691-12562-7 (cl : alk. paper)
1. China—Economic policy. 2. Finance—China. I. Jin, Jing. II. Gao,
Jian. III. Title.

HC427.95.R54 2007
330.951—dc22   2006053170

British Library Cataloging-in-Publication Data is available

This book has been composed in Sabon

Printed on acid-free paper. ∞

press.princeton.edu

Printed in the United States of America

10 9 8 7 6 5 4 3 2 1

Contents

Preface

BECAUSE CHINA IS THE world's largest and most rapidly growing developing country, it is a case study of particular importance and fascination for anyone interested in economic development broadly defined. Not surprisingly, China's economic transformation and development have been much analyzed and debated by both Chinese and foreign economists. The literature on China's economic reform since 1978 is voluminous and generally of a high quality. In this study we draw heavily on that literature in describing the evolution of the economy, the major policy changes, and the debates that emerged about China's overall strategy toward economic reform. In order to make a contribution to this literature we inevitably have had to cover a lot of well-traveled ground, but along the way we offer our own analyses and interpretations of the key issues, some of which may be somewhat controversial—at least we hope so.

The main focus of this book is economic growth in China—what ignited it, what has driven it, what fueled it, and what is needed to sustain it. The book contains two major themes. One is that investment is not only the engine of growth in China, but also the main source of technological progress, productivity growth, and structural change. In developing this argument we provide a critique of conventional growth theory as applied to China. The second theme is that the key to sustaining long-term growth in China is financial sector liberalization and development. We analyze the role of the financial sector in financing investment and the reforms that are needed to improve the functioning of banking institutions and financial markets, which are integrally related. The final chapter of the book shifts the focus to the short run, arguing that investment has not only been the engine of long-term growth, but also the source of boom-bust cycles in

China's economy. We argue that the underdevelopment of the financial sector is not only an obstacle to sustainable long-term growth, but also a source of short-run instability and an impediment to effective macroeconomic stabilization.

We have written this book so as to make it accessible to a broad readership. In this book China experts will find much that is familiar, but perhaps also some interpretations and analyses that are novel. For specialists in the field of economic growth and development we offer an important case study that brings the elegant theory together with the messy reality that is China. Those who work in the field of finance have, in this book, a case study of the consequences of financial repression and the complexities of reforming such a system, which, as this case study makes clear, requires not just changes in policies but an entire reorientation of development strategy. For the lay reader, we offer broad survey of economic policy and performance in China since 1978 that focuses on the key driving forces of past growth and the key challenges to sustaining growth in the future. The book does include technical economic analysis, but we have strived to present it in a way that is accessible to noneconomists. Finally, we have written this book not only for those who are interested in economic policy in general and China in particular, but also for those whose job it is to make policy in China. Policymakers in China no doubt have a deeper knowledge of many of the topics discussed in this book than we do, but we hope they will nonetheless find the overall themes, arguments, and conclusions of the book useful as they debate and formulate economic policy for China's future.

James Riedel
Jing Jin
Jian Gao

Acknowledgments

WE WOULD LIKE TO THANK the China Development Bank and UBS AG (Hong Kong) for generous logistical and financial support. Many people at the China Development Bank contributed to this study, including Liu Jianming, Luo Lin, Li Xiaotao, Sun Longxin, Teng Guangjin, Wu Jingren, and Xie Zhijun, as did many at UBS, including Kath Cates, Vivian Chiu, Annie Cheng, Rory Tapner, Jenny Wong, Boon-cheow Woo, and Joe Zhang. We would also like to thank Wang Xiongjian of the China Economic and Management Academy of the Central University of Finance and Economics. We are especially grateful to Jonathan Anderson, Chief Economist of Asia Pacific at UBS, for allowing us to reproduce a number of the excellent charts that appear in his timely reports on the Chinese economy.

We benefited from extensive discussions with Dr. Guan Shenyi of the China Government Securities Depository Trust and Clearing Company, Rong Zhiping and Zhang Zhijian of the China Development Bank, Yin Jianfeng of the China Academy of Social Sciences, Liu Minhui and Yang Guang of the *China Securities Journal*, Wu Qi of Beijing Securities, and Han Yaqing of the National Council for Social Security Fund.

We would like to thank seminar participants at Peking University, Fudan University, and Zhe Jiang University, in particular Zhang Jun, Zheng Jinghai, Lu Ming, and Wu Guiying, for useful comments and suggestions. Students at the Johns Hopkins University–Nanjing University Center for Chinese and American Studies also offered valuable comments and suggestions on parts of this study. In particular, we would like to thank Huang Yi and Miao Qian, former students at the Hopkins–Nanjing Center, for invaluable research assistance.

We are especially grateful to Richard Baggaley, European Publishing Director of Princeton University Press, for his support and encouragement. We received many useful comments and suggestions from those who anonymously reviewed the manuscript for Princeton University Press, for which we are grateful. Finally we wish to thank W. Max Corden for reading the manuscript and providing invaluable insights and comments.

This study expresses the views and opinions of the respective authors and not necessarily the views of UBS AG or the China Development Bank. The authors are solely and individually responsible for the contents herein.

How China Grows

CHAPTER 1

Overview of Economic Reforms and Outcomes

SINCE THE POLICY reform process began in 1979, China's economy has undergone rapid growth and structural change. If ever there was any doubt that "policy matters," China's experience over the past 25 years should dispel it once and for all. The reforms themselves did not, however, cause growth and structural change, but rather created incentives and institutions, absent in the socialist planned economy, that were a necessary precondition for growth and structural change to occur. It was up to those who participated in the economy—individuals; state-owned, collectively owned, and privately owned firms; as well as government workers and officials—to respond to the newly created incentives and institutions to bring about growth and structural change.

Because the record on growth and structural change in China is remarkable, much effort has been given not only to describing the reforms themselves but also to assessing China's overall approach to reform. No one can dispute that China has been successful, but observers have debated whether an alternative approach to economic reform in China would have yielded even better outcomes than the one chosen. On one side of this debate are those who argue that China's "gradual" and "experimental" approach to reform was appropriate, if not optimal, given the political and socioeconomic conditions that existed at the outset of the reform process (Naughton 1995; Rawski 1994; Lau, Qian, and Roland 2000). On the other side are those who argue that even better outcomes would have obtained if China had avoided experimentalism and instead had more vigorously embraced old-time religion, adopting as quickly as possible the incentive systems and institutions of a typical market economy (Sachs and Woo 2000).

At the heart of this debate is the question of whether China succeeded because of, or in spite of, the gradual, experimental approach it adopted. It has been argued that China's superior performance as compared to other transition economies had far less to do with the gradual, experimental character of the reforms than with the conditions that existed at the outset of the reforms (Riedel 1993; Sachs and Woo 1994). In 1979, after more than a decade of economic and political turmoil, China's economic resources were grossly underutilized and misallocated, with 70 to 80 percent of the labor force in the rural sector largely unemployed or underemployed. From such a starting point, almost any improvement in material incentives was bound to have a significant positive impact on growth and structural change. Proponents of gradualism, however, argue that a more rapid approach would have created many more losers from the reform process who could have generated a political backlash that might have derailed the process altogether. The gradual, experimental approach, the key feature of which was decentralization through a system of contracts between higher and lower levels of government, created incentives and rewards that, so it is argued, co-opted potential adversaries of economic reform into accepting and participating in the process.

This debate is likely to continue for years to come, since it can never be resolved conclusively. It cannot be resolved because the proof on both sides is a counterfactual outcome and as such requires a replay of history. As an ancient Greek philosopher noted, "Even God cannot change the past."[1] For this reason, we avoid weighing in on this debate and instead simply review briefly (in the following sections of this chapter) the basic facts about the reforms and their outcomes. As this review indicates, both characterizations are valid—the reform process was incremental and experimental, while the

---

[1] Agathon, 446?–c.401 B.C., from Aristotle, *Nicomachean Ethics*, VI.2.1139b.

outcome of the process was to bring about the convergence (albeit slowly and still far from complete) of incentives and institutions toward those of a typical market economy. It is also evident from this review that experimentalism is waning, while acceptance of conventional wisdom on market incentives and confidence in their outcomes are gaining ground. Thus the convergence outcome of the reform process, which has been under way for more than two decades and has already fundamentally changed the character of China's economy, is likely to accelerate. Indeed, that outcome is almost guaranteed as a result of China's entry into the World Trade Organization, which effectively locks China onto the convergence path (Woo 2001).

Instead of debating what could have been, we prefer to concentrate on what can be and what is required to make it happen. In this chapter we review past reforms and their outcomes to give perspective on what follows. In chapter 2 we review the literature on the sources of growth in China to identify the driving force of growth and to determine whether it is sustainable. Much of the literature argues that investment, not technological change or total factor productivity growth, has been the driving force of growth in China, but that investment, unlike technological change, cannot be counted on to sustain growth in the future because of diminishing returns to capital deepening. We take issue with this interpretation and argue instead that investment in China has not only been the engine of growth, but also the source of technological progress and structural change. We proceed in chapter 3 to examine the financing of investment through saving in the private, public, and foreign sectors. This examination reveals a glaring weakness that threatens the sustainability of future growth—China's underdeveloped financial sector. In chapter 4 we assess the state of the financial sector, the sources of its weakness and the measures that are needed to allow it to play its increasingly important role in the economy. After 25 years of reform, the emphasis of policy reform must shift from mobilizing unemployed resources and correcting gross inefficiencies to maximizing efficiency in the allocation of China's scarce capital

resources, and nothing is more critical to the efficient allocation of capital than an effective financial system. Chapters 5,
6, and 7 assess the banking sector, bond market, and stock
market and the reforms that have been undertaken to improve the functioning of China's financial institutions and
markets. We observe (in chapter 5) that while the government
has made banking sector reform a high priority and has taken
measure to recapitalize the state-owned banks and improve
their governance, reform of the banking sector is still far
from complete. The government has also acknowledged the
importance of well-functioning bond and stock markets, but
few concrete measures have been taken to achieve this objective. Indeed, we observe (in chapters 6 and 7) that the dominance of state-owned banks in the financial system is also a
major obstacle to the development of the bond and stock
markets in China.

While the main focus of this study is long-term growth, in
the final chapter we shift the focus to the short run. Our aim
in chapter 8 is to explain the ups and downs of the economy.
We give particular attention to the role that government policy, macroeconomic policy in particular, has played in fueling
and dampening major swings in the economy. We argue that
investment has not only been the engine of long-term growth,
but also the source of "boom-bust" cycles in China. Furthermore, we argue that underdevelopment of the financial system is not only an obstacle to sustainable long-term growth,
it is also a source of short-term instability and an impediment
to effective macroeconomic stabilization policy. Ongoing reforms in the financial sector are beginning to moderate the
macroeconomic cycle and make macroeconomic policy more
effective, but further reforms are needed to give policymakers
the tools they need to keep the economy on a high and stable
growth path.

1.1. Agricultural Reform: 1979–85

The term *gradual* has been used to describe China's economic
reform because it proceeded in a stepwise manner. The term is

misleading if it is meant to imply slowness, given that the first step in the reform process transformed, in fewer than five years' time, the dominant sector of the economy. By 1984, agricultural collectives had been replaced by the household responsibility system, under which collectively owned land was assigned to individual households that were free to sell their output at market determined prices after fulfilling their contractual obligation to deliver a portion of output to the state at the government-fixed procurement price. By early 1985, the state had abandoned obligatory procurement quotas in agriculture altogether and replaced them with purchasing contracts between the state and farmers, though there was backsliding on this policy in subsequent years (Lin 1992, 39).

The restoration of family farming and the marketization of agriculture provided powerful incentives to expand production and raise efficiency. The rate of growth of agricultural output increased from 2.9 percent per annum from 1952 to 1978 to 7.6 percent from 1978 to 1984, more than half of which has been attributed to the improvement of incentives that occurred when collective agriculture was replaced with the household responsibility system (Lin 1992). In addition to the household responsibility system, increases in procurement prices and deceases in agricultural input prices also contributed to the expansion of agricultural production, although according to Lin, Cai, and Li (2003, 145) no such changes "made as significant a contribution as the household responsibility system."

The acceleration of growth in the agricultural sector led to increases in real per capita rural income on the order of 15 percent per year for the period 1978–85. Because of a relatively high propensity to save in the rural sector, a significant proportion of the increased rural income was saved in credit cooperatives, put in bank deposits, or invested in new rural enterprises (World Bank 2003, 3). As a result of these investments, the share of employment in agriculture fell from 62 to 53 percent between 1978 and 1985, while the share in rural township and village enterprises rose from 7 to 14 percent (World Bank 2003). Thus, in just five years' time, a major structural transformation was well under way,

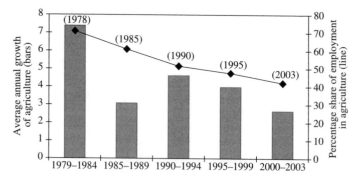

Figure 1.1. Average Annual Growth and the Employment Share of Agriculture, 1979–2003 (percentages). Source: *China Statistical Yearbook* 2004.

one that would continue steadily for the next two decades, although subsequently to be driven by sources other than the growth of agricultural output, which as figure 1.1 indicates never again matched the record of the period from 1978 to 1985.

1.2. Industrial Reform: 1978–93

Agriculture was the obvious place to start the reform process, since it was in the agricultural sector that most people lived and earned their income. The government's top priority, however, was heavy industry, both before and after the reforms commenced. Indeed, the agricultural commune system was designed specifically to squeeze as much surplus out of the agricultural sector as possible to invest in state-owned heavy industry. The commune system was abandoned simply because it did not work either to adequately feed the people or to generate sufficient surplus to shift the center of gravity of the economy from agriculture to industry. The privatization and marketization of agriculture were practical necessities, ideological concessions that were required to further the fundamental objective of industrialization, with heavy, capital-intensive, state-owned industry at the "commanding heights" of the economy.[2] The lack of a comparative advantage in heavy industry dictated a state-led strategy, as is evident from the fact that every other developing country pursuing a similar strategy engaged to some degree in central planning, state ownership of industry, high levels of protection, and industrial subsidies. In China, with its communist ideology, these practices were simply carried to the extreme. When the reforms began in 1978, virtually all industry was owned by the state or by collectives, and so it remained until the early 1990s, when the landmark decision was made to replace central planning with a "socialist market economy" and then subsequently to acknowledge formally the importance of private ownership and the rule of law.[3]

When the reforms began in 1978, it was recognized that industrialization was hampered not only by the failures in the agricultural sector, but also by the poor performance of state-owned industrial enterprises themselves. Thus, concurrently with the reform of the agricultural sector the government began a prolonged, incremental process of reforming state-owned enterprises. The aim of the reforms was to increase the efficiency of SOEs by improving the incentive system. Toward this end, SOEs were given successively greater autonomy in production and investment decision-making and an ever greater share of the profits they generated through a variety of profit remittance contracts and management responsibilities systems.[4]

The reforms undertaken to improve the efficiency and prof-

---

[2] It has been argued that "to a large extent, the displacement of dogmatic ideology in favor of pragmatism was due to a backlash to the Cultural Revolution . . . .They [the leadership] were convinced that without economic development the Party cannot survive, in other words, the necessary condition for maintaining Party's power and regaining popular support is economic development" (Qian and Wu 2000, 12–13).

[3] Both private ownership and the rule of law were finally incorporated into the Chinese constitution in March 1999.

[4] These are described in detail in Lin, Cai, and Li 2003.

itability of SOEs met only limited success, since none adequately resolved the basic principal-agent problem inherent to state ownership. However, other reforms, in particular the dual-track pricing scheme that freed up prices at the margin while maintaining planned prices for SOE quotas, did allow SOEs to participate in China's expanding market economy and led to some improvement in resource allocation in the SOE sector.[5] However, the fundamental problem of low efficiency and profitability in the SOE sector remained. The common view, according to Lin, Cai, and Li (2003, 156), is that "one-third of the country's SOEs incur explicit losses, one-third incur implicit losses, and only the remaining one-third are making profit." Moreover, the losses of SOEs had negative consequences throughout the economy, in particular in the banking sector, where they saddled the state-owned commercial banks with a large stock of nonperforming loans.

Since the mid-1990s, when the bulk of bad loans was accumulated, the government has taken a number of measures to make SOEs more accountable for their profits and losses, as well as to subject them to the threat of bankruptcy and closure. As a result, as figures 1.2 and 1.3 indicate, the number of SOEs has declined by about half since the mid-1990s, and the shares of SOEs in industrial output and employment have declined dramatically.

How then did China achieve an average annual growth rate of 9.2 percent from 1978 to 2004 if the growth effects of the agricultural reforms petered out by 1985 and the reform of state-owned industrial enterprises was only moderately effective? The answer is revealed in figure 1.4, which shows that industrial growth in China was driven by non-state-

---

[5] The dual-track price system is portrayed by some (e.g., Lau, Qian, and Roland 2000) as a Pareto-optimal policy that introduced price flexibility while avoiding political opposition from those who would have lost had price controls simply been abolished. Woo (2001) disputes that China avoided losers because of the dual-track price system and argues that by creating enormous opportunities for corruption, the dual-track price scheme did in fact create social unrest aimed principally at officials who exploited these opportunities.

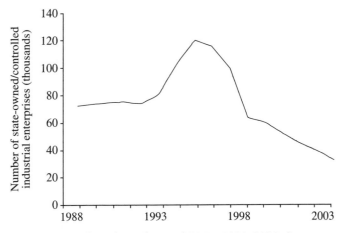

Figure 1.2. Number of Nonfinancial SOEs, 1988–2003. Source: Anderson 2005b, 12.

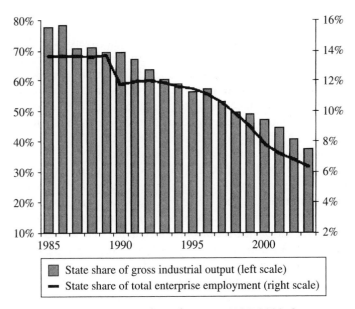

State share of gross industrial output (left scale)
State share of total enterprise employment (right scale)

Figure 1.3. SOE Output and Employment, 1985–2003. Source: Anderson 2005b, 12.

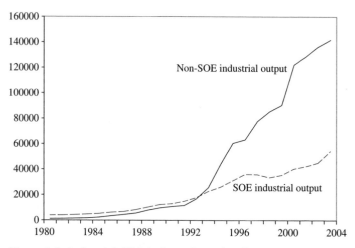

Figure 1.4. Industrial GDP in State-Owned and Non-State-Owned Enterprises, 1980–2003 (RMB 100 million). Source: *China Statistical Yearbook* 2004.

owned enterprises, in the 1980s by the collectively owned rural township and village enterprises and in the 1990s by domestic and foreign privately owned industrial enterprises. Non-state-owned enterprises did not displace state-owned ones, however, since the latter also grew steadily, albeit at rates well below those of collectively owned enterprises in the 1980s and privately owned enterprises in the 1990s.

How was it possible for China to have it both ways—to allow the relatively inefficient state-owned enterprises to continue to expand and, at the same time, to achieve rapid growth in the non-state-owned industrial sector? Two things were necessary for this outcome: (1) a surplus of resources and (2) a set of institutions and incentives that would allow markets to form and resources to flow to the nonstate sector. The first condition, as we have already noted, was met in part by the massive reservoir of unemployed and underemployed labor in the rural sector. The second condition was met by the implementation of a sequence of policy reforms that allowed the formation of markets and provided incentives to undertake economic activity outside the central plan and, after the central plan was abolished in the early 1990s, outside the state sector. The key reform that spurred the growth of the collectively owned township and village enterprises in the 1980s was fiscal decentralization. Administrative decentralization in the late 1970s had shifted managerial jurisdiction over a large number of SOEs to subnational governments. The profit contract system implemented in the early 1980s thus had the effect of allowing a significant proportion of revenue, previously collected by the central government, to accrue to the SOEs and their subnational government owners, who in turn negotiated fiscal contracts with the central government. Subnational governments were allowed to retain revenues they collected above and beyond those they had contracted to transfer to higher-level governments, and in turn were required to finance their own expenditures through self-generated and shared revenues.

One consequence of these measures was to create strong incentives for subnational governments to engage directly in economic activity, leading to the development of rural township and village enterprises, which flourished in the 1980s. Because these enterprises were collectively owned, they were able to skirt the formal and ideological prohibitions against private enterprise. Moreover, since the TVEs operated outside the central plan, they could exploit market opportunities that were excluded in the plan, in particular the production (and ultimately the export) of labor-intensive, light-industrial products in which China, with its abundant supply of labor, had a natural comparative advantage. Because the TVEs received little or no support from the government, they were compelled by competition to strive for efficiency, thus avoiding, at least for a number of years, some of the pitfalls of the SOEs.

1.3. Transition to a Market Economy: 1994–2003

By the early 1990s, the engine of industrial growth in China was running out of steam. The township and village enterprises, in effect, became victims of their own success. As they became more successful, the lack of clearly defined property rights became an issue. As they grew larger, the absence of scale economies became more evident and they became more bureaucratic, acquiring some of the attributes of SOEs (Qian and Wu 2000, 15). Fiscal decentralization, it is argued, created revenue incentives that encouraged subnational governments to engage in protectionist behavior and practice "backward specialization" by duplicating small enterprises across subnational government jurisdictions (Yang 1997). In effect, the centrally planned economy gave way to many regionally planned economies under the control of subnational governments (Young 2000b).

Problems in the SOE sector also intensified over time, and by the early 1990s SOE losses, financed increasingly through bank loans that the SOEs all too often were unable to repay, began seriously to undermine the banking system. In addition, the state found itself, as a result of fiscal decentralization in the previous decade, increasingly unable to control the macro economy, with inflation accelerating and the currency becoming significantly overvalued. In addition to its economic woes, China began in the late 1980s and early 1990s to encounter unprecedented social unrest, fueled by the deteriorating economic situation and public cynicism about official corruption. If all of that were not enough, the collapse of the Soviet Union in 1991 must have helped the leadership realize that the status quo was no longer viable.

Thus the stage was set for a major change in course when the Fourteenth Party Congress met in September 1992, just months after Deng Xiaoping's famous "Southern Tour" to mobilize support for reform even more radical than what had come before. With the Party's endorsement of a "socialist market economy," the leadership began in 1993 to formulate reforms that would replace the fiscal contract system with a tax assignment system that more closely resembled fiscal federalism. Reforms were adopted to recentralize the monetary system, corporatize SOEs, and for the first time acknowledge the private sector as "a supplementary component of the economy" (Qian and Wu 2000, 10). The private sector was upgraded to "an important component of the economy" at the Fifteenth Party Congress in September 1997, and its role formally incorporated in the constitution in March 1999. In addition, in 1994 the dual foreign exchange market was abolished, and in 1996 current account transactions were made fully convertible.

The reorientation of the reform process in the 1990s provided a much needed impetus to industrialization by invigorating the private sector. The share of private firms in industrial output increased from practically nil in the mid-1980s to a majority share of 57 percent by 2004. In the economy as a whole, if one includes the agriculture sector, the private and collective sectors together account for about 75 percent of GDP. The state-owned enterprises sector, on the other hand, still accounts for a disproportionately large share of capital outlays (about 40 percent) and a disproportionately small share of employment (about 8 to 9 percent).

1.4. FOREIGN TRADE AND INVESTMENT

The opening up of China's economy to trade and foreign direct investment has been an important ingredient in the growth of the nonstate sector, particularly in industry, where China possesses a strong comparative advantage in labor-intensive manufactured products. As in other areas of the economy, liberalization of the foreign trade and investment regimes proceeded incrementally, gradually replacing administrative controls on imports and exports with tariffs and quotas and then subsequently reducing tariff rates and abolishing quotas.[6] As figure 1.5 indicates, by the time China entered the WTO in 2001, the average tariff rate had been reduced to 15 percent, and it has continued to decline since then.

In addition to tariff reductions, nontariff barriers have also

[6] See Lardy 2002 for a detailed description of the process of trade liberalization since 1978.

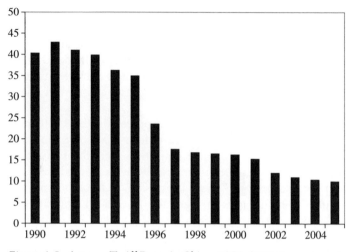

Figure 1.5. Average Tariff Rates in China, 1990–2005 (percentages).
Note: The average tariff for 2005 is the rate committed to in the
WTO. Source: Wu 2004, 96.

been largely eliminated. Import licensing is limited to less
that 4 percent of all imports, and the monopoly of state trading companies was abolished in all but a few sensitive product categories (Lardy 2003, 6). As a result of these measures,
the share of exports and imports in GDP increased from 4.6
and 5.2 percent, respectively, in 1978 to 28 and 26 percent in
2004. Accompanying the growth of trade, the structure of
exports also changed dramatically, with manufactures' share
in exports increasing from about 10 percent in 1978 to 90
percent in 2004.

Foreign investors have had legal status in China since the
reform process began in 1979, but their operations were restricted to equity joint ventures in specific sectors and geo-
graphical regions.[7] Given the government's overriding concern for SOEs, foreign direct investment was encouraged

[7] For a comprehensive survey, see Lemoine 2000.

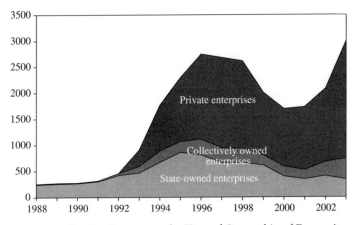

Figure 1.6. Foreign Investment, by Type of Ownership of Enterprise Invested In, 1988–2003 (RMB 100 million). Source: *China Statistical Yearbook* 2004.

mainly in labor-intensive export-oriented industries. Foreign direct investment flourished in the 1990s in part because domestic private companies were constrained, by lack of access to credit and ambiguities about their legal status, from taking up the investment opportunities that were opened for foreign investors (Huang 2005).[8]

Thus, the shift in the orientation of the reform process in the early 1990s had a dramatic impact on the volume and destination of FDI inflows to China. As figure 1.6 indicates, in the 1980s most FDI was in joint ventures with SOEs, while in the 1990s the bulk of it was wholly owned and in joint ventures with private companies. Foreign direct investment has, therefore, not only contributed to growth and industrialization, but also to changing the ownership and production structure of the economy.[9]

[8] This issue is discussed in detail in chapter 3.

[9] By the year 2002, FDI contributed as much as 30 percent to manufacturing production in China (Lardy 2003).

1.5. Financial Sector

The fourth pillar of China's economy, along with agriculture, industry, and foreign trade, is the financial sector, arguably the weakest and, at this stage in the reform process, the most crucial for sustaining growth in the future. Important reforms have been undertaken in the financial sector, including the restoration of a commercial banking system, the emergence of a fledgling bond market, and the establishment of stock exchanges in Shanghai and Shenzhen, and these reforms have not been without success. Several common indicators of financial development have improved dramatically, in particular the ratios to GDP of liquid liabilities of the financial system (M2), bonds outstanding, and stock market capitalization.

When one looks more closely at these and other indicators of financial development in China, as we do in chapter 4, one finds that there is less than meets the eye. For example, the increase in the M2/GDP ratio from 33 percent in 1978 to 190 percent in 2004 is, we argue, as much an indicator of financial repression as it is of financial deepening. The M2/GDP ratio in China is exceptionally high, indeed higher than in almost any other country, precisely because repressive financial policies have limited access to nonbank saving instruments and forced households and businesses to accumulate large savings account balances to meet the cash-in-advance constraint they face due to restrictions on their access to credit. In addition, the increase in the stock market capitalization/GDP ratio is less than impressive when one takes into account the fact that only one-third of outstanding stock is tradable. While government bond issues have grown rapidly, they are almost entirely placed and traded in the interbank market. The corporate bond market hardly deserves the term *market*, since the right to issue bonds is severely restricted and the price of corporate bonds is administratively determined. In the banking sector, interest rates are also controlled, with ceilings on deposit and lending rates at artificially low levels, resulting in an enormous implicit tax on financial saving and non-SOE investment.[10] Thus, we conclude, in chapter 4, that in spite of some positive developments, China's financial system remains highly repressed with deleterious consequences for economic growth. Why does China repress its financial system? In chapter 4, we argue that the reason is the same as for other countries that pursued a heavy-industry-oriented development strategy and repressed their financial systems, because measures that repress the financial system serve the government's development strategy by maximizing the flow of resources to the government and the industrial enterprises it owns. While financial repression serves the government's development strategy, by discouraging financial saving and misallocating scarce capital resources, it does so at a high cost, a cost that is rising dramatically as a result of structural changes that have made the private sector the main engine of industrialization and growth in China. Financial development is crucial for sustaining growth in the future, whereas it was less so in the past, precisely because of this fundamental transformation in China's economy.

We develop this thesis in the following chapters by examining the sources of growth and the role of investment in particular (in chapter 2), the determinants of saving and sources of investment financing (in chapter 3), and the causes and consequences of financial repression (in chapter 4). Chapters 5, 6, and 7 examine the current situation and ongoing reforms in the banking sector, the bond market, and the stock market, in that order. In the final chapter (chapter 8) the focus shifts from the long run to the short run, analyzing the ups and downs of the economy over the past 25 years. We argue in chapter 8 that investment is not only the engine of long-term growth, but also the source of "boom-bust" cycles in China. Furthermore, we argue that the underdevelopment of the financial sector is not only an obstacle to long-term growth, but also a source of short-term instability and an impediment to effective macroeconomic stabilization policy.

---

[10] The ceiling on lending rates was abolished in October 2004, but this measure has yet to have a significant effect on credit allocation in China.

CHAPTER 2

The Source of Growth and the Role of Investment

THIS CHAPTER OFFERS A review and critique of recent studies of the sources of growth in China. Reading these studies, one is struck by how different is the perception of the scale and scope of economic change in China that one gets from casual observation from that which the economist offers up as "statistical reality." Recent studies of the sources of growth in China suggest that there has hardly been any technological improvement over the past two decades, which is belied by everything one sees on the street in terms of the availability of inexpensive consumer goods, the widespread application of the latest information technologies, and the presence of communications towers on every high-rise building. Are we being misled by what our eyes see and our common sense tells us, or are we being misled by the economists' analysis of economic change in China?

2.1. METHODOLOGY OF GROWTH ACCOUNTING

The Solow growth model provides the theoretical framework for growth accounting studies, at the heart of which is the Cobb-Douglas production function:

$$(1) \quad Y_t = A_t K_t^\alpha L_t^\beta \quad \alpha + \beta = 1 \quad A_t = A(0)e^{at} \quad K_T \sum_{t=0}^{T} (I_t - \delta K_{t-1})$$

where Y is real GDP, I is gross investment, K is the real capital stock calculated using the perpetual inventory method with a depreciation rate of δ, L is employment and A is an index of the level of technology or total factor productivity. The exponential terms (α and β) are the elasticities of output with respect to the factor inputs (K and L, respectively) and in the Cobb-Douglas production function have values equal to the income shares of each factor. Expressing equation (1) in logarithms, we get

(2) $\log(Y) = \log(A(0)) + \alpha \log(K) + \beta \log(L) + at.$

Taking the total differential of (2), we get

(3) $dY/Y = \alpha (dK/K) + \beta (dL/L) + dA/A.$

Equation (3) identifies three sources of output growth (dY/Y): (1) capital accumulation (dK/K), (2) employment growth (dL/L) and (3) technological change or total factor productivity growth ($dA/A = a$). The contributions to output growth of capital accumulation and employment growth can be directly measured from published time-series data. The contribution of technological change or total factor productivity growth (TFPG) cannot be observed directly, but can be estimated by either of two methods, both of which have been applied to the China case. One method is to use econometrics to estimate equation (2), interpreting the estimated coefficient on time (a) in equation (2) as the rate of technical change or TFPG. Alternatively, equation (3) can be estimated, in which case the estimated intercept term is interpreted as a measure of TFPG (= dA/A). The other method is to use the period-average growth rates of Y, K, and L (with α and β calculated from the national accounts) to compute dA/A as a residual.

Applying the second method, technological change or TFPG is given by

(4) $dA/A = dY/Y - [\alpha (dK/K) + \beta (dL/L)].$

The bracketed term on the right-hand side is a measure of total factor input growth (TFIG), the weighted average rate of growth of capital and labor. Computed as a residual, dA/A captures not only improvements in technology, but also errors in the measurement of Y, K, and L, changes in the quality of labor and capital, and structural changes that result in the reallocation of labor and capital from sectors of the economy where their productivity is relatively low to sectors where it is relatively high.

2.2. Measurement of TFPG in China

Table 2.1 summarizes the results of several recent growth accounting studies for China. Borenzstein and Ostry (1996) and Hu and Khan (1997) report a real GDP growth rate of 9.2 and 9.3 percent per annum, respectively, while Woo (1998) puts the real GDP growth rate at 8.1 percent over the same period. The difference in these growth rates is due to the application of different base years and different deflators for GDP. It has been argued, and widely accepted, that the official GDP deflator understates the rate of increase of industrial prices and hence overstates the rate of real GDP growth by as much as one to two percentage points (Woo 1998). These errors in measurement of real GDP growth are of course captured in the TFPG residual and hence overstate TFPG by one to two percentage points.

It has also been recognized that published data on employment growth understate the growth of the "effective labor force." Since increases in the educational attainment of the labor force that raise labor productivity are not taken into account, the effect is to understate the contribution of labor and overstate the contribution of TFPG. Several studies (Young 2000a; Wang and Yao 2001) have used published data for the educational attainment of the working-age population in China to construct an index of labor efficiency or human capital (H), which is used to measure the growth of effective labor, the sum of the growth of raw labor and human capital $(dL/L + dH/H)$. Removing the effect of human capital accu-

TABLE 2.1
Accounting for Growth in China (percentages)

Author(s)	Period	dY/Y	dK/K	dL/L	dH/H	TFIG	TFPG	β	δ
Borensztein and Ostry (1996)	1979–94	9.2	9.9	2.7	nc	5.4	3.8	na	na
Hu and Khan (1997)	1979–94	9.3	7.7	2.7	nc	5.5	3.9	45	3.6
Woo (1998)	1979–93	8.1	9.8	2.7	nc	6.3	1.8	50	5.0
Woo (1998)	1985–93	7.5	11.0	2.5	nc	5.9	1.6	50	5.0
Young (2000a)	1978–98	8.1	7.7	4.5	1.0	6.6	1.5	50	6.0
Wang and Yao (2001)	1978–99	9.7	9.4	2.7	2.7	7.4	2.3	50	5.0
Zhang (2003)	1980–98	9.9	9.4	2.8	nc	6.2	3.7	40	na

Note: nc: not calculated; na: not available.

Woo (1998) and Young (2000a) adjust the official GDP growth rates for base-year bias and underdeflation of industrial output. The studies summarized above analyze aggregate GDP growth at the national level in all cases except Young (2000a), who considers only nonagricultural GDP. Definitions: dY/Y: real GDP growth rate; dK/K: real capital stock growth rate; dL/L: employment growth rate; dH/H: human capital index growth rate; TFIG: Total Factor Input Growth; TFPG: Total Factor Productivity Growth; β: labor share of value added; δ: depreciation rate.

mulation from the residual reduces its value by another one to two percentage points.

Average annual TFPG in China for the period 1979–94, as measured in the studies summarized in table 2.1, ranges from a high of 3.9 percent (Hu and Khan 1997) to a low of 1.5 percent (Young 2000a, for nonagricultural GDP). If the GDP growth rates used in Borenzstein and Ostry, Hu and Khan, and Wang and Yao are adjusted downward by one to two percentage points, residual rate of TFPG would be fairly consistent across these studies at about two percent per year, plus or minus a half a percentage point.

Increases in real per capita income derive from increases in labor productivity, the sources of which, in the growth accounting framework, are capital deepening (increases in the capital-labor ratio), human capital accumulation, and TFPG.

TABLE 2.2
Accounting for Labor Productivity Growth (percentages)

Author(s)	Period	Labor Productivity Growth	Contributing Component		
			Physical Capital Deepening (% share)	Human Capital Accumulation (% share)	Total Factor Productivity Growth (% share)
Borensztein and Ostry (1996)	1979–94	6.5	2.7 (41.5)	nc	3.8 (58.5)
Hu and Khan (1997)	1979–94	6.6	2.8 (41.7)	nc	3.9 (58.3)
Woo (1998)	1979–93	5.4	3.5 (65.7)	nc	1.8 (34.3)
Young (2000a)	1978–98	3.6	1.6 (44.4)	0.5 (13.9)	1.5 (41.7)
Wang and Yao (2001)	1978–99	7.0	3.3 (47.6)	1.4 (19.3)	2.3 (33.2)
Zhang (2003)	1980–98	7.1	3.4 (47.8)	nc	3.7 (52.2)

Note: see table 2.1.

Substituting L with (LH) in equation (1), where H is an index of the quality of the labor force, we obtain the following equation for the growth of labor productivity:

$$(5) \quad \frac{d(Y/L)}{Y/L} = \frac{dY}{Y} - \frac{dL}{L} = \alpha \left(\frac{dK}{K} - \frac{dL}{L} \right) + \beta \left(\frac{dH}{H} \right) + \frac{dA}{A}.$$

The growth of labor productivity and its sources, the three components on the right-hand side of (5), as calculated in each of the studies reviewed here, are given in table 2.2.

There is a widespread notion in the literature that increasing labor productivity through capital deepening is inferior to achieving the same outcome through technological change or total factor productivity growth because capital deepening is subject to diminishing returns and will eventually run out of steam, while technological change or TFPG need not (Young

1995; Krugman 1994). Table 2.2 indicates that a significant share of labor productivity growth in China derived from TFPG. Capital deepening (increases in the capital-labor ratio) accounts for less than half of labor productivity growth according to every study other than Woo 1998. Even Young, who has made a career out of debunking East Asia's superlative growth record, gives TFPG credit for about 42 percent of (nonagriculture) labor productivity growth, albeit a relatively low rate of labor productivity growth (3.6 percent per year).[1] If each of the studies summarized here had uniformly taken account of the underdeflation of GDP and the contribution of increasing educational attainment of the labor force, TFPG would have been uniformly found to contribute no more than about one percentage point to labor productivity growth.

2.3. PRODUCTION FUNCTION ESTIMATES OF TFPG IN CHINA

The several recent studies that have used time-series data to estimate a production function for China in order to obtain an estimate of TFPG are summarized in table 2.3. Each of these studies imposes the condition $\alpha + \beta = 1$ (i.e., constant returns to scale) by expressing the model in per capita (more accurately, per unit labor) terms, yielding the following regression equation:

$$(6) \quad \log(Y/L) = c + \alpha \log(K/L) + at + \varepsilon,$$

where c is a constant intercept value and ε is the error term assumed to have the usual properties.

Each of these studies covers the prereform period (1952–79) but omits observations for the period 1958 to 1969, when

---

[1] Young (1995) argues that economic growth in Singapore, Hong Kong, Korea, and Taiwan was mainly due to massive capital accumulation with relatively little contribution from TFPG. Krugman (1994) has interpreted Young's results to suggest that the "Asian Tigers" are in fact "paper tigers."

TABLE 2.3
Production Function Estimates for China (standard errors of the coefficients in parentheses)

Author(s)	Period	Estimate of c	Estimate of α	Estimate of a	R^2 (SEE)	DW
Chow (1993)	1950–57	2.05	0.54	0.005	0.98	nc[a]
	1970–80	(2.88)	(0.43)	(0.019)	(0.05)	
Chow and Lin	1950–57	−0.11	0.65	0.027	0.99	1.62
(2002)	1970–98	(0.127)	(0.04)	(0.004)	0.03	
Li (2003)	1950–57	1.67	0.63	0.027	0.99	0.07
	1970–98	(0.19)	(0.02)	(0.003)	0.04	

Note: Chow and Lin (2002) use the Cochran-Orcutt procedure to eliminate first-order serial correlation in the errors. Li obviously does not make this correction, as the DW statistic indicates.

[a] Not calculated.

the economy was subject to the political upheavals of the Great Leap Forward (1958–62) and the Cultural Revolution (1966–76). Chow (1993), whose study does not extend to the reform period (after 1980), found that there was no TFPG before the reform process began in 1978. Growth of labor productivity in the prereform era (1952–78), which averaged 5.8 percent per year, was entirely due to capital deepening.

Chow and Lin (2002) and Li (2003) incorporate Chow's (1993) finding by setting the value of the trend variable (t) equal to zero for all observations from 1952 to 1978. Their (identical) estimates of a, reported in table 2.3, are therefore the estimated rate of TFPG for the period 1978 to 1998. At 2.7 percent per year, these estimates are within the range of estimates for TFPG obtained in the growth accounting studies reviewed above. Their data indicate that the average annual rate of growth of output per worker was 6.7 percent, while the average annual rate of growth of capital per worker was 6.2 percent. It follows that TFPG (at 2.7 percent per year) accounted for 40 percent of the growth of labor productivity, while capital deepening accounted for the remaining 60 percent. If, however, these studies had taken account of underdeflation of GDP and increases in educational attainment of the labor force, TFPG would all but disappear.

2.4. EXPLAINING TFPG IN CHINA

As noted in the introduction to this chapter, perceptions of the scope and scale of economic change in China that one gets from casual observation and those that are derived from statistical analysis of Chinese data are vastly different. Some economists suggest that what they offer is only the "statistical reality," but that is not entirely accurate.[2] Economic data must be analyzed within the framework of a theoretical model—or as economists sometimes say, a fact is not a fact without a theory. An economic analyst looks at the world through the lenses of an economic model, which in the case of the studies summarized above is the Solow growth model. If the model is valid and the data are reasonably accurate, then perhaps what the economists offer may be regarded as the "statistical reality." If, however, the model is questionable, then so too are the statistical results based on it. A critique of the China growth accounting studies must therefore include a critique of the underlying model used in the analyses as well as whatever doubts one may have about the data.

It was not by accident that rate of investment increased, total factory productivity began to rise, and the structure of the economy began to change only after the reform process began in the late 1970s. At the root of it, the most fundamental cause of economic change over the past two decades is the reform process that led to the marketization of the economy and its integration into the international division of labor (Woo 2001, 108). It is commonly held, however, that policy reforms that make the economy more efficient, raising the rate of investment as well as the rate of return on investment, do not lead to higher growth in the long run because of diminishing returns to capital investment, a key feature of the Solow growth model.

[2] For example, Young 1995, 2002.

As Borensztein and Ostry (1996, 226) argue: "the improvement in material incentives [from the reforms] which served to boost measured productivity growth in the 1980s and 1990s is more in the nature of a level than a growth effect." It is worth noting, however, that even within the Solow model the growth effects of policy reform, while eventually petering out because of diminishing returns, can persist for decades.[3] Of course, if one abandons the Solow model in favor of an endogenous growth model, in which the return to investment does not diminish with the accumulation of capital, then policy reforms that improve material incentives permanently raise not only the level of output but the long-run growth rate as well.

This key property of the Solow model—diminishing returns to investment—together with the implicit assumption of the model that capital is a homogeneous input, from which it follows that investment is simply a process of adding to the stock of the same old machines used decades ago, explains why analysts of economic change in China imply that capital accumulation is an inferior source of growth and emphasize instead the importance of technological change. In the case of China, however, most studies also discount the contribution of measured TFPG, where the growth effect of technological change shows up. Borensztein and Ostry (1996, 226) strike the common theme of these studies: "Although TFP has made a remarkable contribution in the post-reform period, there are reasons to believe that true underlying productivity growth, in the sense of technical progress, is substantially lower." If not technological change, what then is measured in the TFPG residual? The answer is what these studies refer to as "the usual suspects"—the transfer of labor out of agriculture; within the industrial sector, the transfer of labor out of state-owned enter-

---

[3] Assuming reasonable values for the parameter of the Solow model, the growth effects of a reform that increases saving and investment rates or economic efficiency diminish at about 4 to 5 percent per year, which means that only half of the growth effect of reform will have been exhausted after about 18 years (Jones 1998). If human capital is incorporated into the model, increasing the income share of total (physical and human) capital, then under reasonable assumptions the growth effects diminish at half that speed, raising the half-life of the growth effect to about 35 years (Mankiw, Romer, and Weil 1992).

TABLE 2.4
Accounting for the Labor Reallocation Effect (percentages)

Period	GDP Growth Rate	Labor Productivity Growth Rate	TFPG	Labor Reallocation Effect	Net TFPG
1979–93	8.1	5.4	1.8	1.1	0.7
1985–93	7.5	5.0	1.6	1.3	0.3

Source: Woo 1998.

prises and into the more dynamic non-state-owned enterprises; increases in educational attainment; and rising participation rates in the labor force.

Each of the studies summarized above acknowledges that measured TFPG captures the effect of reallocation of labor from agriculture, where its productivity is low, to industry, where it is significantly higher. Woo (1998) alone provides a measure of the reallocation of labor effect, though he does not attempt to explain its underlying cause. Instead, he models the reallocation of labor from agriculture as an exogenous and independent source of growth.

Woo's calculation of the labor reallocation effect, reported in table 2.4, yields a contribution to growth of 1.1 percent per year for the period 1979 to 1993 and 1.3 for the period 1985 to 1993. Deducting the labor reallocation effect from TFPG renders it almost inconsequential, no more than about 0.7 to 0.3 percent per year. The effect of capital reallocation from agriculture and within industry from state-owned enterprises into more dynamic TVEs was not calculated because of lack of reliable data; nevertheless it is certain that such effects if they were measured would further diminish TFPG. Woo also does not measure the effect of increases in labor effectiveness from increases in the educational attainment of the workforce, which if deducted from his measured TFPG would further reduce the contribution of technological change and in all likelihood make it negative.

The positive rates of TFPG reported in the studies summarized in table 2.2 would all but disappear if the effects of (1) underdeflation of industrial output, (2) labor reallocation from agriculture, and (3) increases in the educational attainment levels of the workforce were uniformly taken into account. If, in addition, these studies uniformly were to take account of the effects of reallocation of labor from state-owned enterprises to the more dynamic TVEs, the effects of capital reallocation from agriculture and, within industry, from state-owned enterprises, then the measured rate of TFPG in China over the past two decades would surely be found to be negative in each and every one of these studies. The "statistical reality" offered by the growth accounting studies summarized here is that the level of technology in China has not increased and in all likelihood has regressed. What we see, we are not to believe!

2.5. The Contribution of Investment Reconsidered

As this review of the literature reveals, much effort has been given to making downward corrections in the measured rate of TFPG in China over the past two decades. None of the studies reviewed here has given any consideration to the possibility that the contribution of investment has been miscalculated and in all likelihood understated. If, for example, we ask the simple (and crucially important) question of what generated the reallocation of labor from agriculture, the counterpart of which is the relatively rapid growth of employment in industry since 1980, especially in nonstate industrial enterprises since the early 1990s, is not the answer investment? If that is correct, then it is not appropriate to model the reallocation of labor effect as an exogenous source of growth—it is instead endogenously determined by the rate of investment in the industrial and commercial sectors.

Indeed, the argument can be made that not only labor reallocation but overall employment growth in China is endogenously determined by investment, for this is a logical implication of a widely accepted interpretation of the transition experience of China. The argument has been made that what differentiates the transition experiences of Russia and Eastern

Europe, on the one hand, and China, on the other, is not the pace of reform (gradualism versus "big bang"), but instead key differences in the initial structure of their respective economies (Riedel 1993; Sachs and Woo 1994; Woo 1999). The Soviet Union and Eastern Europe started the transition from a centrally planned to a market economy with about 90 percent of the labor force employed in state-owned enterprises (Woo 1999). China began the process with most (about 80 percent) of its labor in the rural sector, much of it unemployed or underemployed. In order to build a new, more efficient industrial sector, Russia had to tear down its old, state-owned industry to free up resources for the new economy. China, on the other, did not have to do this—because of its reservoir of surplus labor in the rural sector, it could build a new and efficient labor-intensive, export-oriented light industrial sector side-by-side with its old, capital-intensive, state-owned industrial sector. Indeed, such was (and to a lesser extent still is) the vastness of its reservoir of unemployed labor that it could even expand the state-owned industrial sector while at the same time building a dynamic labor-intensive nonstate sector.[4]

This key structural feature of the Chinese economy on the eve of its transition to a market economy—the presence of a vast reservoir of under- and unemployed labor—has important and heretofore overlooked implications for growth accounting. It implies that the conventional assumption that the growth of employment is exogenously determined by demographic and other labor supply factors does not hold in China. In China, with its vast reservoir of unemployed labor, employment growth in general, and in particular in the industrial and commercial sectors, was (and perhaps still is) determined endogenously by

---

[4] Figure 1.1 (in the previous chapter) illustrated this process in China. Starting from a small base in 1978, the industrial output of nonstate enterprises, mainly TVEs, has grown to overtake the state-owned enterprises, its share in industrial GDP rising from about 22 percent to about 78 percent between 1979 and 2001. Non-state-owned industry did not expand at the expense of state-owned industry, for throughout the period from 1978 onwards the state-owned industry also expanded at a respectable rate (about 8 percent per annum from 1978 to 1998).

the rate of investment in industry and commerce that created the jobs that were largely filled by migrant workers from the rural sector.[5]

The dependence of employment growth and reallocation on investment is not the only source of underestimation of investment's contribution to growth. An even greater source of underestimation derives from the conventional practice of treating capital as if it were a homogeneous input. The conventional practice, followed in each of the studies summarized above, is to deduct from gross investment 5 or 6 percent of the capital stock of the previous year as depreciation. The implicit assumption is that 5 percent of the capital stock wears out every year and must be replaced with identical capital just to keep the capital stock intact. This practice implies that a dollar of depreciation reduces output as much as a dollar of new investment adds to it. If, however, firms replace old capital not because it wears out, but instead because it becomes economically obsolete due to technological changes that raise real wages and change other relative prices in the economy, then firms must replace obsolete capital with new and improved capital assets— replacing old obsolete capital with new obsolete capital would hardly make business sense and certainly would do nothing to restore profitability. Deducting depreciation from gross investment in measuring its contribution to growth is simply wrong and understates the contribution of investment.[6] Put another

[5] Official labor force growth rates will not reveal this salient fact because, as is well known, the official rate of unemployment is grossly understated, and in addition no account is taken of underemployment, especially in the rural sector, where it is rampant.

[6] The growth accounting framework uses the growth of the capital stock,

$$\left(\frac{dK}{K}\right)_t = \frac{I_t - \delta K_{t-1}}{\sum_0^t (I_t - \delta K_{t-1})},$$

to measure the contribution of capital accumulation to growth. This is an accurate measure of the capital stock even when depreciation is from obsolescence, since obsolescence does reduce the value of the capital stock and so must be taken into account in measuring the capital stock over time, as in the way, when capital depreciates because of obsolescence, scrapping it entails no social cost and should not be netted out of gross investment in measuring investment's contribution to growth, a point that has been made over the years by a number of experts on national income accounting.[7]

What proportion of the capital wears out each year and what proportion becomes obsolete is unknown. The studies summarized above set the depreciation rate, seemingly arbitrarily, at 5 percent (in Young's study at 6 percent). Implicitly, all depreciation is assumed by the growth accounting studies to be due to wear and tear, and its replacement is therefore deducted from gross investment. Studies of capital depreciation, however, indicate that most, if not all, depreciation is due to obsolescence (see Scott 1989, 30, and the sources cited therein). If most of depreciation is from obsolescence, then the growth accounting studies for China summarized above have understated the contribution of investment and overstated the TFPG

---

denominator above. It is not, however, an appropriate way to measure the contribution of investment to growth, since the deduction of depreciation due to obsolescence in the numerator implies there is a social cost to scrapping obsolete capital assets, which there is not.

[7] This point has long been recognized as the following quotations, taken from Scott (1989, 33), reveal. Kuznets (1974, 156) asks, "In what sense does obsolescence justify a deduction from capital, from the standpoint of society, however much it may be justified by business firms as protection against loss of relative competitive position vis-à-vis newcomers who can reap the differential advantage of their newness?" And he answers, "There is something absurd in a procedure that reduces the value of a capital good that is physically otherwise unimpaired because there has been technical progress." Ruggles and Ruggles (1956, 1140) write, "Technological progress frequently does destroy the earning power, and thus the money value, of already existing capital goods, and this type of obsolescence should and does enter into the depreciation allowances of businessmen. But technological progress causes no real loss to the economy as a whole." Usher (1980, 105) makes the same point: "Obsolescence, for example, can be looked upon as the result of a transfer of wealth from owners of old types of machines to owners of new types of machines, labor, or consumers. The loss to the firm is genuine but the loss to the economy is counterbalanced by gains elsewhere."

residual by about 2.5 percentage points.[8] Taking everything into account, therefore, it is hard to escape the conclusion that, as interpreted within the framework of the Solow growth model, technology in China has been regressing at a rate of about 3 percent per year. Such a conclusion is of course absurd, but hardly more absurd than to suggest that it has been zero, which is the logical conclusion of the growth accounting studies summarized above, albeit one that each of the studies has avoided making. Seeing, after all, is believing!

2.6. TECHNOLOGICAL CHANGE RECONSIDERED

Dissatisfaction with the Solow model's treatment of technological change as an exogenous determinant of growth has led to a new generation of "endogenous" growth models. Currently a large number of competing models in the literature endogenize the process of technological change by making it a function of all kinds of different activities and expenditures, such as learning-by-doing (the proxy for which is the capital stock), expenditure on research and development, human capital accumulation, and so forth. Often it is hypothesized that such activities are subject to increasing returns and involve positive externalities, implying that suboptimal levels of technology-generating expenditures will obtain unless the government subsidizes them.

If we reject the assumption of the Solow model that investment is simply the reduplication of capital assets, then it is obvious that among the different expenditures that contribute to technological change, investment has to be one of the most important, especially in a transition economy like China's that started out from a position far below the frontier of technology. The marketization and internationalization of the economy that began around 1980 have given China the

[8] A depreciation rate of 5 percent reduces the rate of capital accumulation by an equivalent 5 percent. If the capital share of income (α) is 0.5, then the contribution to growth of investment is understated by 2.5 percentage points and the TFPG residual is overstated by an equivalent amount.

opportunity to acquire new technologies from abroad by investing in imported machinery and equipment that embody the latest technology and by attracting foreign investors that have superior managerial and production know-how, and who, through a joint ventures and demonstration effects, can pass that know-how on to domestic Chinese firms. In addition to the various foreign sources of technological change that have been opened up, China's reforms have also created an incentive, indeed an imperative, for domestic firms to change the way they operate to achieve and maintain competitiveness in domestic and world markets. All such changes in method of operation, whether they take the form of purchasing new and better machines or adopting new and improved management and accounting systems, entail a cost—an investment expenditure. To quote Samuel Johnson, "Change is not made without inconvenience (i.e., cost), even from worse to better."[9]

According to this view, which comes mainly from Scott (1989), technological change and investment are part and parcel of the same thing. Changing technology requires investment, and investment inevitably involves technological change. Indeed, in a dynamic market economy in which technology is continuously changing, investment is necessary to maintain the value of the firm in response to the continuous process of obsolescence caused by technological progress and the changes in relative prices that it brings about. Since technological change and investment are for practical purposes inseparable, it does not make sense to proceed as if they were separable, as growth accounting does.

We share Scott's view that "without investment there is no growth." How much growth a given amount of investment will generate is quite another matter, however, and can vary widely across countries and over time depending on the quality of a country's economic infrastructure broadly defined. Economic infrastructure here refers not only to physical infrastructure, but also to the government's policy framework, the country's corporate governance and legal systems, and its

---

[9] *The Concise Oxford Book of Quotations*, 2nd ed. (1981), 134.

economic institutions that influence investment decision making, including the financial system and product and factor markets generally (Scott 1989, 177). All of these factors that together influence the quality of a country's economic infrastructure determine the efficiency of investment. The efficiency of investment and the level of investment operate, according to this view, interactively to determine the rate of growth, not separately as in the growth accounting framework. Scott's view is instead that improvements in the economic infrastructure increase growth because they raise the social (and often the private) rate of return on investment and as such are persistent, not once-and-for-all effects as in the Solow model.

Scott has expressed this view in the form of a growth equation that takes the following form:

$$(7) \quad g = a \cdot \rho \cdot s + b \cdot g_{LA},$$

where g is the rate of growth, a and b are constants, ρ is an index of investment efficiency as determined by the quality of the broadly defined economic infrastructure, s is gross investment spending as a share of GDP, and g_{LA} is the growth of employment adjusted for change in the educational attainment of the workforce.[10] In this model there is no residual to account for technological change or TFPG because it cannot be measured separately from investment. The growth of output (or value added) is fully accounted for by the growth of quality-adjusted employment, the rate of investment (s), and changes that occur over time in investment efficiency. In this framework policy reforms that improve material incentives have not only level effects, but also growth effects that are sustainable as long as the policy reforms themselves are sustained. In this model the return to investment is constant over the long run, not because exogenous technological change offsets diminishing returns, as in the Solow model, but because investment itself changes the world and creates and reveals

---

[10] This equation is derived in Scott 1989, chapter 6, and in Riedel 2003, where it is applied empirically to explain the growth of the manufacturing sector in Taiwan.

new investment opportunities. Thus, if we want to understand growth in China, we must understand first and foremost what determines the level and efficiency of investment.

2.7. POSTSCRIPT: INVESTMENT VERSUS DOMESTIC DEMAND AS A SOURCE OF GROWTH

In mid-2005, after several years of debate, the government embraced a policy aimed at reducing China's dependence on investment as a source of growth and relying more on domestic consumption (Wen 2005).[11] Unfortunately, this debate, and the recently announced shift in strategy, lacks a sound basis in economics. Since aggregate supply and demand (ex-post) are by definition equal, GDP growth measures both the growth of supply (output) and demand (expenditure, domestic and foreign). In the short term, fluctuations in expenditure can and do affect the growth rate, as is explained and analyzed in chapter 8. However, in the long run, growth is supply driven, mainly as a result of investment and investment-generated improvements in technology and productivity growth. If, in the long run there is an acceleration of domestic consumption expenditure, then for this to generate sustainable growth the level and composition of output will have to change, which will require investment. One can debate the relative merits of a strategy that relies more or less on domestic, as opposed to foreign, demand, but there is no basis for suggesting that domestic consumption can replace investment as the main source of long-term growth. The fact is, without investment there can be no growth in the long term, no matter what the source of demand.

[11] This postscript is added to address the comments of an anonymous reviewer who suggested that our emphasis on the importance of investment was out of step with government policy in China.

CHAPTER 3

Saving and the Financing of Investment in China

IF INVESTMENT IS the driving force of economic growth, technological progress, and structural change in China, as we have argued in the previous chapter, then the next logical question is what drives investment. The simple answer is saving, since it is only through saving that resources are made available for investment. Since saving is what makes investment possible, we are led to the further question of what drives saving. This chapter examines the sources of saving in the Chinese economy and assesses whether and to what extent they are sufficient in quantity and allocated across alternative investment opportunities with sufficient efficiency to sustain growth in the future.

Investors in China and elsewhere rely not only on their own savings, but also on the savings of others in the economy to finance their investments. When investors draw on savings other than their own, mainly the savings of households, it is mostly done through the financial system, which in the case of China is dominated by the state-owned commercial banks. It follows, therefore, that the quantity and quality of investment to a large extent depends on how effectively the financial system mobilizes and allocates the nation's pool of saving.

In addition to savings funneled through the domestic financial system, some investors also receive financing directly from the government. The government in China saves and borrows in financial markets not only to finance investment in "public capital"—economic infrastructure and other so-called public goods—but also to finance in part the investments of state-owned enterprises. Since government saving derives from taxation, it inevitably involves the crowding out of private savings. Furthermore, when government borrows to finance investment, it also inevitably crowds out private investors in financial markets. The level and efficiency of investment depend, therefore, not only on the effectiveness of the financial system, but also on the tax and spending policies of the government.

In addition to private and public domestic saving, investors also get financing from abroad, in the case of China mainly through foreign direct investment. International financial markets also provide a mechanism for investing the nation's savings abroad. In the 1990s, the outflow of Chinese savings vastly exceeded the inflow of foreign investment, placing China in the anomalous position of being a net creditor in the world economy. That the world's fastest-growing, capital-scarce economy, presumably with one of the highest rates of return on investment in the world, is a net creditor in the world economy is a paradox that demands an explanation, and in the final section of this chapter, one is provided.

The examination, in this chapter, of the sources of saving and the mechanisms by which saving is allocated among alternative investments reveals a glaring weakness that threatens China's future growth—the financial system. China's financial system, in spite of recent progress, remains fragile and underdeveloped. As a result, it plays a relatively small role in mobilizing and allocating the nation's savings. Moreover, because it is weak and underdeveloped, to the extent that it does mobilize and allocate savings, it does so relatively inefficiently. We leave it to subsequent chapters to examine the sources of inefficiency in the financial system and the measures that need to be taken to allow the financial system to play its increasingly important role in generating and sustaining economic growth in China. Here our aim is to identify the problem and assess its implications for investment and growth.

3.1. INVESTMENT

Gross Domestic Investment

Investment as a share of GDP has been exceptionally high ever since the beginning of the reform process in 1978. Real gross domestic investment over the entire period averaged a fairly steady 37 percent of real GDP. The rate of gross domestic *fixed* investment, on the other hand, has increased significantly in recent years, rising from an average of 29 percent of real GDP from 1978 to 1993 to an average of 36 percent since then. As figure 3.1 indicates, the rate of fixed investment has increased without a proportionate rise in the rate of gross domestic investment because of a significant decline in the rate of inventory accumulation since 2000.

Until the year 2000, inventory accumulation amounted to, on average, about 6 percent of GDP. That meant that about 18 percent of gross domestic saving had to be devoted to financing inventories rather than to increasing the productive capacity of the economy. The high rate of inventory accumulation in China is generally attributed to the government's policy of requiring SOEs to maintain and expand employment even though they were unable to sell a significant proportion of what they produced. Reforms that increased competitive pressure on SOEs, both from trade liberalization and from the expansion of the private sector, exacerbated the problem. Since 1997, however, the government has allowed SOEs to reduce employment to improve profitability, while at the same time state-owned commercial banks have become less willing to give SOEs unlimited working capital to finance inventories (Shirai 2001, 55; Lardy 2003, 12). As a result, since the mid-1990s, employment in SOEs has declined (see figure 3.2) and a larger share of domestic saving has been made available for fixed investment.

Investment in Fixed Assets by Ownership

Gross domestic fixed investment in China is virtually equivalent to what is reported in the *China Statistical Yearbook* as

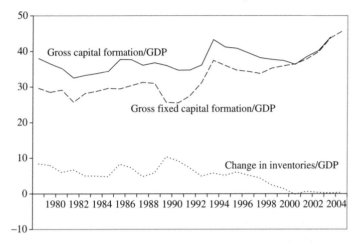

Figure 3.1. Gross Domestic Investment and Its Components as a Percentage of GDP, 1978–2004. Source: *China Statistical Yearbook 2005.*

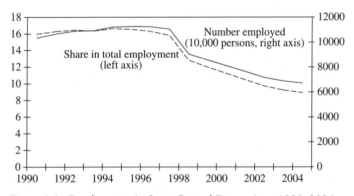

Figure 3.2. Employment in State-Owned Enterprises, 1990–2004. Source: *China Statistical Yearbook 2005.*

"investment in fixed assets." These data are useful because they classify investment according to ownership: state-owned units, collectively owned units, individuals' enterprises (including family farms and small private businesses), and other types of ownership (including joint-ownership enterprises, shareholding

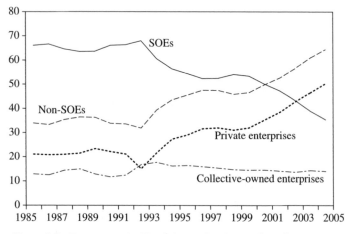

Figure 3.3. Investment in Fixed Assets by Ownership Share, 1985–2004 (percentages of Total Investment in Fixed Assets). Source: *China Statistical Yearbook* 2005.

companies, joint-venture enterprises, and foreign-owned companies).

As figure 3.3 indicates, until the early 1990s, SOEs accounted for the bulk of fixed investment. Since then, fixed investment by non-state-owned enterprises has outpaced SOEs and since 2000 has surpassed the level of fixed investment by SOEs. As figure 3.3 indicates, private enterprises (defined here as the sum of individuals' enterprises and "other") by 2004 invested somewhat more than did the SOEs.

The decline in SOEs' share in fixed investment is a significant positive development, given the widespread perception that the return on investment in the state-owned enterprises is far below the private sector. It is nonetheless worth noting that, at 35 percent of total fixed investment, the SOEs' share is still about four times higher than their share in total employment (8.5 percent in 2004). Thus, while the center of gravity of the economy is beginning to shift from the SOE sector to the private sector, a major imbalance in the allocation of resources between the public and private sectors remains.

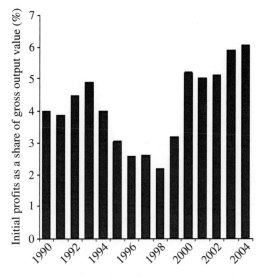

Figure 3.4. Industrial Profit Margins, 1990–2004.
Source: Anderson 2005e, 2.

The Return on Investment

The fall in SOE employment in absolute numbers, not just as a share of the labor force, and the decline in recent years of inventory accumulation, would seem to point to an improvement in the efficiency and profitability of SOEs at least since the late 1990s. In addition, the reallocation of labor and capital from the SOE sector to private enterprises should also have raised the average rate of return in the business sector, since it is widely maintained that the return on private investment greatly exceeds that of the SOEs.

Lacking data on the capital stock for the corporate sector, we are unable to compute the rate of return on capital. However, since measures of the economy-wide capital stock indicate that the capital-stock-to-GDP ratio in China has been roughly constant (Chow and Lin 2002; Li 2003), as a proxy for the trend in the rate of return we use the ratio of before-tax operating surplus to gross output in the industrial sector. Figure 3.4 indicates that industrial profit margins have increased signifi-

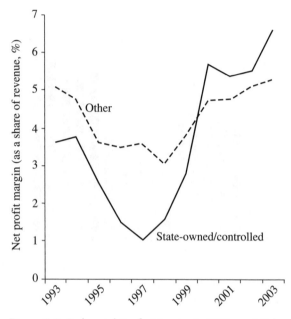

Figure 3.5. Industrial Profit Margins in SOEs and Other Enterprises, 1993–2004. Source: Anderson 2005b, 26.

cantly since 1998 and remained high even after the investment-growth cycle peaked in 2003 (discussed in detail in chapter 8). Moreover, the improvement in the average industrial profit margin is not only due to the growing importance of private enterprises in the industrial sector, but also, as figure 3.5 indicates, to rising rates of return in the SOE sector as many of the more inefficient and unprofitable firms were closed down, merged, and sold off after the downswing of the 1992–96 investment-growth cycle (discussed in detail in chapter 8).

3.2. FINANCING INVESTMENT

The sources of financing of fixed in investment in China from 1981 to 2004 are shown in figure 3.6. Perhaps the most striking feature of investment financing in China is the predominant

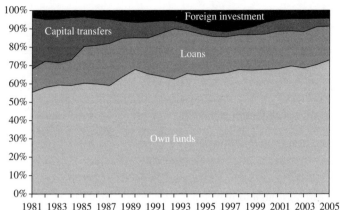

Figure 3.6. Source of Finance of Fixed Investment, 1981–2004 (percentages). Source: *China Statistical Yearbook* 2005.

role of "self-financing," which consists mainly of retained earning, funds raised through bond issues and in informal financial markets, and other sources. Loans from the banking system finance only about 20 percent of total investment, with capital transfers from the government budget (7 percent) and foreign investment (4 percent) accounting for the remainder.

The sources of financing of aggregate fixed investment mask significant differences in the sources of investment financing by enterprises of different ownership status—the state-owned, collectively owned, and private firms. As table 3.1 indicates, self-financing is the single largest source of investment finance for all three types of enterprises, though it is significantly more important for collectively owned and private enterprises (73 and 57 percent, respectively, in 2003) than for state-owned enterprises (51 percent). Nevertheless, major changes have occurred over the past decade in investment financing, especially for private enterprises. Before the early 1990s, self-financing was virtually the only source of finance for private investment, since private companies had little or no access to bank loans and other forms of formal finance. As the legal status of private companies began to improve in the 1990s with the official endorsement of a socialist market economy

TABLE 3.1

Investment Financing by Ownership and the Distribution of Loans by Ownership, 1988–2003 (percentages)

	1988–1992	1993–1997	1998–2002	2003
State-Owned Enterprises				
Retained earnings and informal finance	54.1	64.4	60.4	50.6
Loans	25.4	24.3	23.8	25.6
Capital transfers from government	11.6	5.0	10.7	10.4
Foreign investment	8.9	6.6	2.9	1.6
Collectively Owned Enterprises				
Retained earnings and informal finance	65.5	66.8	77.5	72.7
Loans	31.8	24.7	12.6	11.6
Capital transfers from government	0.4	1.4	5.4	4.2
Foreign investment	2.3	7.2	4.5	5.0
Privately Owned Enterprises				
Retained earnings and informal finance	96.9	70.7	77.0	56.6
Loans	3.1	12.8	16.9	21.5
Capital transfers from government	0.0	0.3	0.5	0.4
Foreign investment	0.0	19.5	11.4	7.2
Distribution of Loans				
State-owned enterprises	75.6	63.6	59.8	46.1
Collectively owned enterprises	21.3	19.0	9.2	7.7
Privately owned enterprises	3.1	17.4	31.0	46.2

Source: *China Statistical Yearbook*, various issues.

(at the Fourteenth Party Congress in 1992), the implementation of a "grand strategy" of a rule-based market economy in 1993, and the official recognition of the key role of private enterprise at the Fifteenth Party Congress in 1997, private companies began to get limited access to bank credit, though as of 2003 bank loans still financed only 22 percent of private sector investment, and private borrowers received only 46 percent of total investment credit. The state-owned enterprises, whose share in industrial output is much lower than private enterprises, still obtain a disproportionate share of investment loans, though there is a clear indication that this imbalance is being rectified.

Another major change over the past decade is the destination of foreign financing of investment, which before the early 1990s was mainly directed to state-owned enterprises. Since the early 1990s, however, foreign financing of fixed investment has flowed in growing volume predominantly to private companies, as is illustrated in figure 1.6. It should be noted, however, that a significant part of the bulge in foreign investment in the private sector in the mid-1990s likely represents domestic private investment, which reportedly flowed out of China to Hong Kong only to return disguised as foreign investment so as to qualify for the preferential tax incentives, greater access to bank loans, and better protection of property rights accorded to foreign-invested companies.[1]

3.3. FINANCIAL FLOWS BETWEEN SECTORS

While self-financing is the single largest source of investment finance in China, a significant share of investment is financed externally through intersector financial flows. The national income accounts provide a framework for identifying the sources of external finance. GNP (the sum of GDP and net factor income receipts) is identically equal to the sum of public and private consumption (C) and investment (I) expenditure and the balance on the current account of the balance of payments (CAB):

(1) $GNP = C + I + CAB.$

GNP is also identical to the sum of consumption expenditure (C) and domestic saving (S). Thus, the national income accounting identity can be equivalently written as

(2) $I = S + F,$

[1] This issue is taken up in more detail below.

where $F = -CAB$ is the change in net foreign liabilities of the private and public sectors, including the change in net foreign official reserve assets of the central bank. As such, F is a measure of the net inflow of foreign savings.

The national income accounts of China provide a breakdown of consumption and investment expenditure by sector (public and private), but do not report a comparable breakdown of income by sector; hence it is not possible to derive saving by sector from the national income accounts. The flow-of-funds data available for the years 1992 to 2002 do provide such a breakdown for four sectors of the economy: (1) public and private nonfinancial enterprises (E), (2) public and private financial institutions (FI), (3) households (H), and (4) central and local government (G).[2] Using these data, the saving-investment accounting identity (equation 2) can be decomposed as

$$(3) \quad (S_E - I_E) + (S_{FI} - I_{FI}) + (S_H - I_H) + (S_G - I_G) + F = 0.$$

Figure 3.7 presents the saving-investment balances for each sector for the period 1992–2000.[3] As figure 3.7 reveals, the net financial deficit of the enterprises sector is mainly financed by the financial surplus of Chinese households. Government is also a net saver, though on a much smaller scale. Foreign savings, as figure 3.7 shows, have not been a significant source of investment finance in China, and indeed have been negative every year other than 1993, the counterpart of which is China's surplus on current account of the balance of payments. The large inflows of foreign direct investment in the 1990s have been more than offset by portfolio capital

---

[2] The flow-of-funds data are in the *China Statistical Yearbook* with a three-year lag. Hence, the most recent flow-of-funds data (*China Statistical Yearbook* 2005) are for the year 2002.

[3] The saving-investment balance of financial enterprises is not reported in figure 3.4 since the financial enterprises contribute insignificantly to intersector financial flows. The influence of financial institutions mainly derives from how well they perform the role of intermediating between household savers and investors in enterprises.

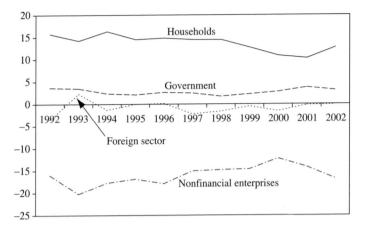

Figure 3.7. Saving-Investment Balances by Sector, 1992–2002 (as a percentage of GDP). Source: *China Statistical Yearbook* 1999, 2000–2005.

outflows and increases in official reserves assets of the central bank (discussed in detail below).

3.4. HOUSEHOLD SAVING

As noted above, households have become a principal source of saving in the Chinese economy since the reform process began in 1978. Before 1978, household income was low and only a small proportion was saved. Instead, saving derived mainly from the planned surpluses of state-owned enterprises, which flowed to the government to finance planned investment expenditure. Since 1978, household saving has increased steadily, reaching a high of 21 percent of GNP in 1995 and 1996, and accounting for a large share of total domestic saving.[4] Since the

---

[4] It would be preferable to relate household saving to disposable household income rather than GNP. Unfortunately data on disposable household income are not available for the entire period. Since 1990, however, household saving expressed as a percentage of disposable income and GNP exhibit a similar pattern (Kuijs 2005).

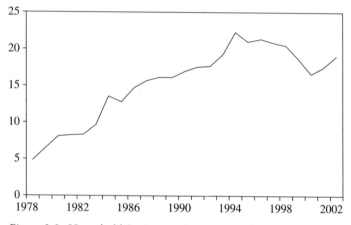

Figure 3.8. Household Saving as a Percentage of GNP, 1978–2002.
Source: Kraay 2000 (1978–95) and the *China Statistical Yearbook*
(thereafter).

mid-1990s, as figure 3.8 indicates, household saving as a percentage of GNP, while still high by international standards, has
declined.[5]

Since households are a major source of investment financing
in China, the apparent decline in the household saving rate
since 1996 is a matter of considerable importance for China's
future growth prospects. After rising steadily for two decades,
why did the household saving rate in China begin to decline in
the mid-1990s? Some tentative answers to that question can be
found in past studies of Chinese household saving behavior,
which find that it conforms remarkably closely to the predic-
tions of the conventional theory of saving.

The key determinant of the household saving rate, according
to theory, is per capita income. For example, in the Keynesian
model, consumption (C) is modeled as a function of income

[5] Saving rates are reported in figure 3.8, from 1978 to 2002, measured by
changes in aggregate stocks of assets held by households. This measure of
household saving is adopted here because it matches closely the household
saving rate obtained from the flow-of-funds data for household income and
expenditure.

(Y)—specifically, $C = a + bY$, where a is interpreted as the subsistence level of income and b is the marginal propensity to consume $(0 < b < 1)$. It follows that saving $(S = Y - C)$ is also a function of income $[S = -a + (1 - b)Y]$, and further that the rate of saving (S/Y) rises with income $[S/Y = -(a/Y) + (1 - b)]$. An implication of the Keynesian theory of consumption is that there exists a virtuous circle whereby higher income leads to more saving, hence more investment and higher growth, which in turn leads to higher income. This virtuous circle has clearly operated in China, as figure 3.8 indicates and as econometric estimates of the household saving function for China confirm (Modigliani and Cao 2004; Kraay 2000; Wakabayashi and MacKellar 1999; Qian 1988).

The key variable working in the opposite direction on the Chinese household saving rate is the migration of the population from the rural to the urban sector. The population shift to the urban sector exerts a negative influence on the household saving rate because the saving rate among rural households has been on average about three times higher than among urban households (Kraay 2000, 11).[6] This difference reflects different institutional and social environments in the rural and urban sectors. As has been noted, "Urban households enjoy access to highly subsidized housing, education and health care benefits, and most are covered by generous (although unfunded) pension schemes through their employers. In contrast, few rural households enjoy these benefits, and most rely on their own saving and their children for support in old age" (Kraay 2000, 12).

As figure 3.9 indicates, an increasing proportion of income accrues to urban households, both because of the migration of the population from the rural to the urban sector and because of the widening income gap between rural and urban households. Thus, while total household disposable income in the urban sector was about half of total rural household

[6] A recent study (Kuijs 2005) suggests that the divergence between rural and urban saving rates has declined in recent years, though as late as the mid-1990s the rural saving rate was apparently two or three times higher than in urban areas.

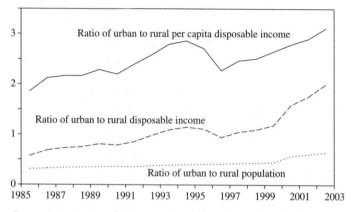

Figure 3.9. Ratios of Urban to Rural Population, Per Capita Income, and Disposable Income, 1978–2002. Source: *China Statistical Yearbook* 2004.

income in 1978, by the year 2002 it was twice that of the rural sector. The population shift and the growing per capita income gap between rural and urban households, given the significant difference in savings rates between these two sectors, can be expected to have a significant negative impact on the overall household saving rate, especially in recent years, when the ratio of urban to rural disposable income increased dramatically.

In addition to per capita income and the rural-urban migration, several other determinants of saving rates have been featured in the literature on household saving behavior in China. Several prominent studies have focused on expected future wealth as the key determinant of the household saving rate (Qian 1988; Kraay 2000; Modigliani and Cao 2004), on the premise that Chinese households adjust the rate at which they save so as to maximize intertemporal welfare. Unfortunately, households' expectations of future wealth are not observable; hence these studies use ex-post measures of future growth as proxy for expected future wealth on the assumption that households' expectations are rational and hence accurate on average. While the theory behind these studies is elegant, the reality in China is not, in particular because of the absence in China of a well-developed financial system that provides the means whereby households may smooth consumption over time so as to maximize intertemporal welfare.

Other potential determinants of household saving include the age-dependency ratio, uncertainty about future income, and financial sector development. These variables are also difficult to measure directly, and their relationship to the rate of saving is in some cases ambiguous. For example, financial sector development that improves households' access to credit, by easing the household budget constraint, may reduce households' propensity to save for major expenditures. On the other hand, financial development, by making a broader array of financial assets available for household investment, may increase the propensity to save. Since it is not our purpose here to test alternative theories of saving, but instead simply to try to explain the data on the household saving rate, we rely on the two primary explanatory variables—per capita income and rural-urban migration. It turns out, as we show below, that these two variables alone fully explain the year-to-year variation in China's household saving rate.

The decline in the household saving rate since the mid-1990s suggests that the negative influence of rural-urban migration has, since the mid-1990s, outweighed the positive effect of rising real per capita household income. Here we estimate a household saving function to test that hypothesis. It seems likely that the impact of both the rise in per capita income and the fall in the rural-urban population ratio would diminish over time, which we allow for by introducing these two variables in quadratic as well as linear form. Thus, the saving function to be estimated is specified as

(4) $S/Y = a_0 + a_1 \cdot \log(RPCY) + a_2 \cdot \log(RPCY)^2$
$\quad + a_3 \cdot URPR + a_4 \cdot URPR^2 + \varepsilon,$

where S/Y is the household saving rate, $\log(RPCY)$ is the log of real per capita GNP, $URPR$ is the urban-rural population ratio, and ε is the error term and is assumed to have the usual

TABLE 3.2
Estimate of Regression Equation (4): Dependent Variable: Household Saving as a Percentage of GNP

Variable	Coefficient	t-statistic
Constant	−4.4	−5.9
Log of per capital GNP	1.68	5.5
Log of per capita GNP squared	−0.13	−5.4
Urban-rural population ratio	−2.8	−3.3
Urban-rural population ratio squared	2.5	3.1

$$R^2 = .98 \quad F = 179.3 \quad DW = 2.2$$

Data source: See figure 3.8 for S/Y and China Statistical Yearbook otherwise.

properties. The hypotheses mentioned above predict a negative sign for a_0, a positive sign for a_1, a negative sign for a_2, a negative sign for a_3, and a positive sign for a_4. The results, using annual data for the period 1978–2002, are presented in table 3.2.

As table 3.2 indicates, the two determinants of the household saving rate (in linear and quadratic form) together explain 98 percent of the year-to-year variation in the household saving rate in China. Over the period, the average elasticity of the saving rate with respect to per capita income is about 1.7, implying that a 10 percent increase in per capita income led to a 17 percent increase in the saving rate. However, as the (negative) coefficient a_3 indicates, the effect of rising per capita income on the saving rate diminishes with successive increases in per capita income. Moreover, the values of the coefficients on per capita income (a_1 and a_2) indicate that the positive effect of rising per capita income on the household saving rate had by the year 2002 largely been exhausted. The coefficient for the urban-rural population ratio is negative, as expected, and the coefficient on the quadratic form of the variable is positive, indicating that the negative impact of rural-urban migration diminishes as an ever larger proportion of the population takes up residence in the urban sector. As figure 3.10 indicates, the model fully explains the rapid rise and subsequent decline in the household saving rate, confirming that

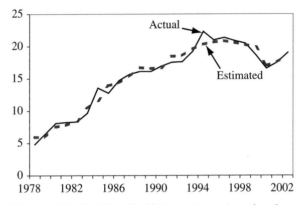

Figure 3.10. The Household Saving Rate: Actual and Estimated (percentages of GNP).

since 1997 the negative impact of rural-urban migration has dominated the positive impact of rising per capita income.

The results reported above have important implications for China's future growth prospects. Since the reforms began, household saving has been an important source of investment finance. As table 3.3 indicates, households have financed enterprise investment mainly through the banking system, which in the mid-1990s received about 90 percent of household financial saving. Since the mid-1990s, a growing share of household financial saving has been placed in other financial assets, mainly government bonds, which as discussed below have become the main source of government budget deficit financing, some significant part of which has resulted from large capital transfers to state-owned enterprises (discussed below). If the household saving rate continues to decline, as is likely, the rate of investment will also likely decline and with it the growth rate.

Whether measures should be taken to avoid such an outcome is problematic. Indeed, the recently announced policy of the government is to encourage households to spend more and save less. The economic logic of this policy is, however, not at all clear. A preferable approach, in our view, would be

TABLE 3.3
Household Saving and Investment in China, 1992–2002 (percentages)

	1992–95	1996–99	2000	2001	2002
Household saving rate	30.9	29.7	25.5	25.4	31.2
Saving in real assets/total	25.7	29.4	33.5	35.6	31.5
Saving in financial assets/ total	74.3	70.6	66.5	64.3	68.5
Currency/financial assets	15.7	5.5	10.2	8.7	9.8
Bank deposits/financial assets	76.1	76.4	67.8	99.4	106.3
Securities/financial assets	10.9	19.6	22.8	19.0	11.3
Other plus E&O	–2.7	–1.5	–0.8	–27.1	–27.4

Source: Flow-of-funds data, *China Statistical Yearbook* 1999–2003.

to liberalize the financial system, giving firms and households more access to bank credit and financial markets and giving the market more freedom to determine financial prices (interest rates and stock and bond prices), allowing households themselves to determine how much to save, based on sound incentives, whether that amount is higher or lower than in the past.

3.5. GOVERNMENT SAVING AND INVESTMENT

Assessing the role of government as a saver and investor, and therefore as a source of economic growth in China, is extremely difficult. Measuring government saving, the difference between government revenue and current expenditure, is straightforward, but measuring government investment is not. A major complication arises because government investment data do not differentiate capital transfers to state-owned enterprises that produce goods and services sold in the market from government investment in economic infrastructure and other public goods, which in many cases are not priced or sold in a market.

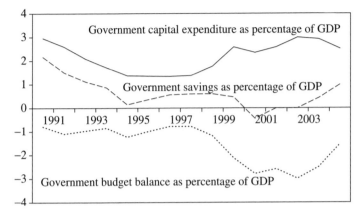

Figure 3.11. Government Saving and Investment as a Percentage of GDP, 1991–2004 (national income accounts). Source: *China Statistical Yearbook* 2005.

As figure 3.11 indicates, government investment, defined in the *China Statistical Yearbook* as "expenditure for capital construction," including capital transfers to state-owned enterprises, exceeds government savings by an amount that grew to the equivalent of about 3 percent of GDP by 2000, the counterpart of which is the government budget deficit, financed for the most part by issuing domestic currency government bonds.

The only source of data that allows one to identify government capital spending separate from capital transfers to SOEs is the flow-of-funds data (1992 to 2002). As figure 3.12 indicates, government capital spending, excluding capital transfers to SOEs, most of which is presumably invested in economic infrastructure and other branches of public goods, is one to two percentage points of GDP less than government savings. It follows, then, that government transfers to SOEs, which ran about 3 percent of GDP until 1999 and 2000, when they rose to 5 percent of GDP, are financed in part through tax revenues and through the issuance of government debt to households and financial institutions. Financial institutions obtain the revenue with which they purchase government

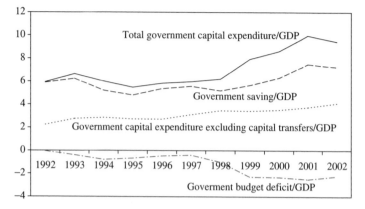

Figure 3.12. Government Saving and Investment as a Percentage of GDP, 1992–2002 (flow-of-funds data). Source: *China Statistical Yearbook* 2005.

bonds mainly from household bank deposits, which further underscores the importance of households as the main source of investment financing in China.

The distinction between government investment in SOEs producing private goods and investment in infrastructure and other public goods is important in assessing government's contribution to growth. It is now recognized that private goods and services sold in the market are generally more efficiently produced by private enterprises, which is of course the main rationale for privatization of SOEs. State ownership in the public goods sector is another matter, since what defines public goods and services is the failure of the market to produce them, or at least to produce them efficiently. Indeed, market failure in the public goods sector defines the central role of government in a market economy. Government's contribution to growth hinges largely on how well it fulfills its essential role of supplying infrastructure and other key public goods and services.

Unfortunately, assessing government's contribution to growth through the provision of public goods and services is extremely difficult. One of the difficulties in assessing the contribution to economic growth of public spending on infrastructure is that it has both positive and negative effects on private saving and investment and hence on growth. The financing of government capital spending, either through taxation or public borrowing, has a negative effect on growth because it inevitably crowds out private saving and investment. On the other had, the provision of economic infrastructure can have a significant positive effect on the return to investment in the private goods sector, thereby raising the rate of growth that obtains from any given level of investment. For example, if government spending is financed entirely through taxation at a flat rate of t, the rate of growth (within the growth model proposed in the previous chapter) is given by

$$(5) \quad g = r \cdot s(1-t) + \lambda g_L = \phi(\sigma,t) \cdot s(1-t) + \lambda g_L$$
$$\text{where } r = \phi(\frac{G_I}{Y}), \, \sigma = \frac{G_I}{G} \, t = \frac{T}{Y},$$

where s is the private saving and investment rate, t is the flat tax rate, G is government spending equal to government revenue (T), σ is the share of capital spending (G_I) in total government spending $(= G_I/G)$, λ is the labor share of value added, and g_L is the growth of quality-adjusted employment. Assuming the rate of return (r) is a positive and diminishing function of government capital spending on infrastructure as a share of GDP $[r = \phi(G_I/Y) = \phi(\sigma \cdot t)]$ government spending and growth exhibits an inverted U-shaped relationship, as illustrated in figure 3.13.[7]

As figure 3.13 suggests, for any given value of $\sigma > 0$, government spending initially has a positive effect on growth through its impact on the rate of return to private investment, though eventually the negative crowding-out effect dominates. It is hardly surprising, therefore, that there is little solid econometric evidence on the impact of government spending on growth, since most econometric studies test for a linear re-

[7] For purposes of this illustration we assume the rate of return is related to the tax rate (t) and the share of capital spending to total government spending (σ) as $r = \phi(\sigma \cdot \tau) = r_0 + \sigma(a_1 \cdot \tau - a_2 \cdot \tau^2)$, where $a_1 = 1$, $a_2 = 0.5$, $r_0 = 0.1$, and $s = 0.25$.

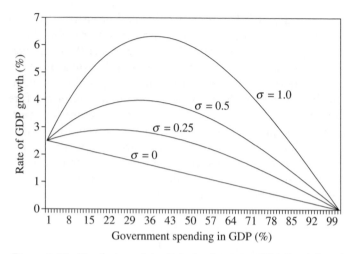

Figure 3.13. Simulation of the Relation between GDP Growth and the Share of Government Spending in GDP for Different Values Sigma.

lationship between the share of government spending (G/Y) and economic growth. In our view, the preferable approach to analyzing the impact of government spending on growth is to focus on the impact of capital spending on the rate of return to investment in the private-goods sector. The stock of public capital, like the policy framework, legal and financial systems, and product and factor markets generally, is part of the economic infrastructure, broadly defined, that determines the efficiency of investment and hence the rate of growth that the nation's savings generate.

Unfortunately, the data required to analyze the effect of government investment in infrastructure on the rate of return are not readily available.[8] What information we do have indicates that government infrastructure investment is about 20

---

[8] While most empirical studies of this issue test for the effect of government spending on growth, Aschauer (1989a, 1989b) demonstrates the positive impact of government capital spending on the return to investment in the United States. Riedel (1992) obtains a similar finding for a cross-section of developing countries.

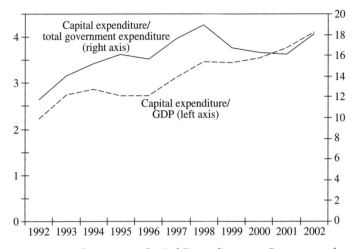

Figure 3.14. Government Capital Expenditure as a Percentage of Total Government Spending and GDP (using flow-of-funds data). Source: *China Statistical Yearbook* 2005.

percent of total government spending and about 3 percent of GDP, both of which ratios have been rising in recent years, as figure 3.14 indicates. Clearly government investment in SOEs constitutes a major diversion of government financial resources that could potentially be used to expand the stock of infrastructure capital, raise the return on investment, and increase growth. Thus, in addition to raising efficiency, privatization of SOEs increases the capacity of the government play its key role in a market economy—supplying public goods.

It must be recognized, however, that government investment in infrastructure is not the same thing as creating productive infrastructure capital. The value of private capital is measured by the profits it generates, while the value of public capital is measured by what it costs to create, not by the benefits that society derives from it. Indeed, it has been suggested that "in a typical developing country less than 50 cents of [public] capital were created for each public dollar invested" due to inefficiency, corruption, and waste in the public sector (Pritchett 1996, n.p.).

In the case of China, only a few studies have attempted to measure the value of public infrastructure capital in terms of its impact on productivity and growth. One study, using provincial panel data, found that the stock of public capital, measured by the cumulative stock of investment in transportation, storage, postal services, and telecommunications, is a statistically significant determinant of cross-provincial productivity differences (Fu, Vijverberg, and Vijverberg 2004). A second study, also using provincial data, but based on physical measures of the stock of infrastructure capital (transportation network density, per capita output of coal and electricity, and telephones per 1,000 persons), reached a similar finding—"differences in geographic location, transportation infrastructure, and telecommunications facilities do account for a significant part of the observed variation in the growth performance of provinces" (Demurger 2001, 115). While these studies confirm that government infrastructure investment has raised productivity and growth, they do not provide a basis for determining whether the benefits from government capital spending justify the costs in terms of private saving and investment crowded out by public investment.

3.6. Foreign Saving

As noted above, China is in the anomalous situation of being a net saver in the world economy. Typically, capital-scarce developing countries are debtors rather than creditors in the international financial system, especially countries like China that are net oil importers and growing very rapidly. The net outflow of Chinese saving is measured by the current account of the balance of payment, which as figure 3.15 indicates has been in surplus every year since 1990 with the exception of 1993. In 2004, for example, the current account surplus was $69 billion, or about 4 percent of GDP, which means that just over 10 percent of Chinese savings were invested abroad.[9]

---

[9] Unless otherwise noted, monetary amounts are U.S. dollars. Some studies put the level of "capital flight" from China as high as 12 to 25 percent of domestic saving in China. See Gunter 2004 and Sicular 1998.

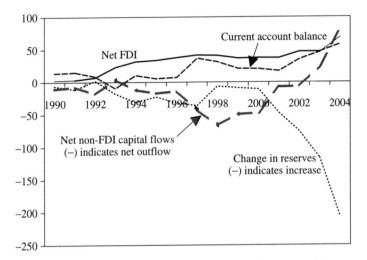

Figure 3.15. The Balance of Payments, 1990–2004 (U.S. dollars billions). Source: International Monetary Fund, *International Financial Statistics*, 2005.

The magnitude of the net outflow of domestic savings, it has been argued, is vastly understated in the published balance-of-payments statistics due to rampant underinvoicing of exports and overinvoicing of imports that are undertaken to evade controls on capital outflows (Gunter 2004). Using partner-country data for 22 of China's main trade partners, Gunter estimates that China's trade and current account surpluses are as much as four times greater than reported in official Chinese balance-of-payments statistics. The cumulative current account balances from 1990 to 2004, according to official statistics, total $329 billion; adjusted for misinvoicing following the method used in Gunter (2004), they would add up to more than $1 trillion. If one adds to this amount the cumulative net inflow of foreign direct investment since 1990 (about $487 billion), then net non-FDI capital flows amount to about $700 billion (net outflow), which is matched by the cumulative increase in foreign reserves since 1990 of about $700 billion. Even according to official statistics, the net outflow of portfolio capital from 1990 through 2004 is exceptional, amounting to about $300 billion. Since 2002, net non-FDI capital flows have reversed direction in anticipation of an appreciation of the Renminbi, giving China large surpluses in both current and capital accounts, the counterpart of which is the enormous recent buildup of foreign reserves. Whether all or part of the net portfolio capital outflow from China can legitimately be termed "capital flight," as some have suggested (e.g., Sicular 1998; Gunter 2004), is open to debate. What is not in question, however, is that about 10 percent, and perhaps as much as 20 percent, of national saving since 1990 has been diverted from domestic investment and instead invested in world financial markets.

The anomalousness of China's balance-of-payments situation is underscored by the fact that at the same time China was investing somewhere between 10 and 20 percent of its saving abroad, foreigners were making major direct investments in the productive capacity of the economy. Over the period from 1990 to 2004, $381 billion of foreign direct investment flowed into China, while at the same time somewhere between $300 and $600 billion of portfolio capital flowed out. What explains the demand in China for foreign assets when the return on domestic investment is presumably several times higher than what can be earned in international financial markets?

Several hypotheses have been advanced to explain this anomaly; at the root of each of them is the weakness and inefficiency of the Chinese financial system.

Weak aggregate demand. A current account surplus is identical to the excess of national income over domestic expenditure (public and private consumption and investment). In spite of measures taken to stimulate domestic consumption and investment expenditure after 1996 through successive cuts in interest rates, the surplus on current account has persisted. Woo (2003, 11) attributes the persistence of current account surpluses and the marked deflationary pressures in the economy after 1997 to "the absence of adequate financial intermediation in China." The government's increased pressure on state-owned commercial banks to reduce the ratio of nonperforming loans led to constraints on lending to SOEs, while at the same time lending to the more profitable non-state enterprises was hindered because of uncertainty about their legal status and difficulties in evaluating their creditworthiness (as noted above). As result, the most dynamic and profitable enterprises in the economy are forced to save after-tax earnings in order to invest, which imparted a deflationary bias in the economy and led to chronic current account surpluses. As Woo (2003, 16) argues, "The right solution to the problem of excess saving is not for the government to absorb it by increasing its budget deficit, but to establish an improved mechanism for coordinating private saving and private investment."

Institutional bias in favor of foreign-invested enterprises and against domestic enterprises. Trade surpluses and the large inflow of foreign direct investment provide the foreign exchange that allows Chinese savings to be invested abroad. The argument has been made, however, that a significant share of foreign direct investment, in particular the 50 percent of total FDI that goes into labor-intensive manufacturing for export, "should be properly cast as an outcome of the poor efficiencies of China's financial system" (Huang 2005, 132). The argument is that much of the FDI that occurs in China's export-oriented industries only happens because of financial biases against domestic private companies, which under other circumstances could have satisfied the world's demand for Chinese labor-intensive manufactures just as efficiently through contract arrangements with foreign buyers. However, because of their weak legal status (weaker indeed than that of foreign enterprises in China) and biases in the financial system that make it difficult if not impossible for private companies in China to obtain financing for investment and working capital, equity financing via FDI has became the dominate mode of production and exporting in China. Thus, Huang concludes, "Although the effect is efficient, at its core, what labor-intensive FDI has done is to offset some of the massive inefficiencies in the Chinese system." Its contribution to the Chinese economy, he suggests, "is fundamentally ameliorative, not additive." Indeed, in support of this general conclusion, it has been suggested that as much as 25 percent of FDI in China in the early 1990s is accounted for by recycled domestic investment—Chinese investors moving money offshore (mainly to Hong Kong) and then bringing it back into the country disguised as foreign investment in order to qualify for special incentives designed to attract foreign investment, including tax concessions and special arrangements for retaining and repatriating foreign exchange (Sicular 1998, 9).

The low return to savers versus investors. The presumption that the social rate of return on investment in China exceeds the return on financial assets in international markets is surely warranted. At the aggregate, economy-wide level, the rate of return (r) can be approximated by the following equation:

$$(6) \quad r = \frac{g_Y - \lambda \cdot g_{LA}}{I/Y},$$

where g_Y is the growth of GDP, λ is the labor share of national income, g_{LA} is the growth of the quality-adjusted labor force, and I/Y is the ratio of gross investment (I) to GDP (Y). Assuming values for the variables in (6) that are more or less consistent with the values for China in recent years ($g_Y = 0.08$; $\lambda = 0.5$; $g_{LA} = 0.02$; and $I/Y = 0.35$), implies an average rate of return in China of about 20 percent, though it is likely that the average for private enterprises is significantly higher than 20 percent and for state-owned enterprises is significantly lower than this overall average. In any case, the average across the economy is certainly many times higher than the return in international financial markets.

The answer to the puzzle, we suggest, is at least in part the enormous spread that exists between the return that investors earn (on average around 20 percent) and the return that savers earn in the banking system. Households, the principal savers in Chinese system, earn an annual interest rate on their deposits (in 2004) that ranges from 0.72 percent on demand deposits to 3.6 percent for five-year savings deposits.[10] Enterprises, which account for about 40 percent of deposits in the banking system, mainly for the purpose of amassing capital for investment, earn a similarly low rate of interest. The enormous spread between the returns to savers and investors is clear evidence of the inadequacy and inefficiency of the system of financial intermediation in China. It is very likely that the strong latent demand for external financial assets on the part of Chinese savers derives at least in part from the low return they earn on their bank deposit savings, given the not insignificant risk they face on these assets from the weakness and fragility of the banking system, saddled as it is with a high ratio of nonperforming loans. The spread between the return to saving and to investing constitutes an enormous tax on saving and investing, which not only encourages the outflow of capital, but also discourages saving and investment domestically.

3.7. SUMMARY AND CONCLUSIONS

China's growth record since the beginning of the reform era in 1978, summarized in chapter 1, is stellar. Nevertheless, most studies of the sources of growth have suggested that China's achievements are less impressive because investment, rather than technological change or total factor productivity growth, has been the driving force of growth. In chapter 2 we took issue with this interpretation, arguing that it derives from the misguided application of an inappropriate model of economic growth. We do not question the importance of investment for economic growth in China—to the contrary, we argue that it has been all-important. What we take issue with is the notion that technological change and productivity growth occur independently of investment. In our view, investment is the principal means by which China has raised its level of

---

[10] *China Statistical Yearbook* 2005, 676.

technology and dramatically changed the structure of its economy, thereby raising per capita income. To understand past growth and arrive at an assessment of future growth prospects, we argue, one must understand the underlying determinants of investment. Since saving is what makes investment possible, we have examined in this chapter the sources of saving in China and the process through which savings are allocated across alternative investments. This examination has revealed a key weakness in China's economic system that threatens future growth—the underdevelopment of the financial system.

The underdevelopment of the financial system is revealed in many of the key features of the saving-investment nexus in China. We observe that the financial system plays a relatively small role in mobilizing and allocating savings. The enterprise sector in general, and the increasingly important nonstate enterprise sector in particular, rely predominantly on "own funds" to finance investment. Bank loans constitute a major share of investment financing only for the relatively inefficient and unprofitable state-owned enterprises. Because they are inefficient and unprofitable, the state-owned enterprises have saddled the banking system, in particular the dominant state-owned banks that are required to lend to them, with a large stock of nonperforming loans.[11] The banking system's ineffectiveness in intermediating between saving and investment in the past was mainly the result of the government's policy of mandating banks to support state-owned enterprises. Now that that policy is changing and banks are being encouraged to make loans on a commercial basis, the banking system's ability to improve the process of financial intermediation is severely crippled by the erosion of its capital base as a result of the bad loans it made in the past. In an effort to improve its asset portfolio, banks have begun to reduce the proportion of credit extended to state-owned enterprises and

[11] According to a recent World Bank (2004, 75) study, "Non-performing loans have been estimated at about 25–30 percent of total loans outstanding for the state commercial banks and higher for the rural credit cooperatives, city commercial banks and policy banks."

lend more to private companies. However, this change has benefited private borrowers less than it might have because banks have at the same time absorbed a large proportion of government debt issues.

The saving-investment nexus is hampered not only by the weakness and inefficiency of the financial system, but also by the government's fiscal policy. The government finances its spending through a combination of taxation and borrowing, both of which have the effect of crowding out private sector saving and investment. The crowding out of private saving and investment may be justified if the government's spending contributes sufficiently to expanding the stock of "public capital," the infrastructure and other public goods and services that are required to make the economy work efficiently, but which because of their public-good attributes are not supplied, or not supplied efficiently, by the market. Unfortunately the proportion of government resources devoted to public capital spending is significantly lower than it would otherwise be because of the large capital transfers the government makes to help finance the state-owned enterprises. Thus, the heavy bias in the banking system in favor of the least creditworthy borrowers, the state-owned enterprises, is further reinforced by the government's spending policies. Through both mechanisms, the banking system and the government budget, the nation's savings are disproportionately channeled to the state-owned enterprises at the expense of the more efficient and profitable private firms.

In spite of these shortcomings, China has achieved high rates of investment and growth. Certainly much of the credit must be given to Chinese households, which responded to the material incentives brought about by economic reforms to save a growing share of their disposable income. From a very low saving rate before 1978, household saving increased to an amount equivalent to about 20 percent of GNP by the mid-1990s. Since then, however, the household saving rate has been declining. We have put forward and tested the hypothesis that the rising rate of household saving was the product of a virtuous circle of rising saving leading to rising income, which in turn led to higher rates of saving. Since the mid-1990s, how-ever, this virtuous circle has been broken, as we suggest, by population migration from the rural sector, where saving rates are high, to the urban sector, where saving rates are much lower. If the falloff in the rate of household saving continues, as is likely, it will mean lower rates of investment in the future. Whether measures should be taken to avoid this outcome is problematic. What is clear, however, is that the incentives that guide household saving should be improved through financial sector reform. Currently the financial saving of households is done almost entirely in the banking system, where it earns in-terest rates that are one-tenth or less the return on investment. Liberalizing interest rate policy and developing alternative sav-ing instruments through the development of corporate stock and bond markets offer great opportunities for improving the incentives that determine household saving in China.

The low rate of return to savers and the lack of alternative saving instruments in China not only distort the incentive to save, but have also encouraged savers to invest a significant share of their financial saving abroad. We find that anywhere from 10 to 20 percent of domestic saving is invested in for-eign financial markets rather than in expanding the produc-tive capacity of the Chinese economy. As a result, China is in the anomalous position of being a net creditor in the world economy, in spite of the fact that the return on investment in China is many times higher than in world financial markets. The opportunity cost in terms of domestic investment fore-gone from the large outflows of Chinese savings can be re-dressed, we argue, only by an aggressive policy of financial sector development. Imposing restrictions and tougher penal-ties on capital outflows may be effective in the short run, but in the longer term, economic incentives predominate. The key to solving the capital outflow problem is, therefore, to im-prove the return on saving and offer a wider array of finan-cial instruments in which to save at home.

One might reasonably ask why we emphasize the impor-tance of financial sector development for sustaining growth in the future, when in the past China achieved extraordinary growth with only limited financial sector development. The answer to this question is surely that conditions in the Chinese economy today are very different from those that existed at the outset of the reform process 25 years ago. At that time, the country had just emerged from more than a decade of political and economic turmoil, the result of which was that a vast proportion of the nation's resources were underutilized and grossly inefficiently allocated. From such a situation, even modest improvements in the system of incentives brought enormous gains. Today, after 25 years of reform, a large proportion of the previously underutilized resources have been absorbed in productive activity, and many (though by no means all) of the gross inefficiencies in the system have been corrected. As a result of these changes, the importance of efficiency in the allocation of China's scarce capital resources is of utmost importance for sustaining growth, and nothing is more critical to the efficient allocation of capital than an effective financial system.

CHAPTER 4

Financial Sector Repression

THE PREVIOUS CHAPTER put forward the argument that China's underdeveloped financial system is the main threat to the sustainability of future growth at rates comparable to those of the past two decades. Though relatively less important in the past, financial sector development is crucial for growth in the future because China's economy has fundamentally changed over the past two decades. The state-owned industrial sector, which was, and still is, the main beneficiary of China's underdeveloped, state-controlled financial system, currently contributes a relatively small proportion of industrial production. The private sector has become the main source of industrialization and growth, but its access to external finance through the financial system is extremely limited. Furthermore, the government-imposed controls and restrictions that distort the intermediation process also reduce the volume of intermediation by discouraging savings through the financial system. As a result, a growing share of China's dwindling savings is being invested in real property and in foreign financial markets instead of in expanding the productive capacity of the economy.

This chapter examines China's financial sector. It addresses the following questions: (1) Why do countries like China repress their financial systems? (2) How repressed is China's financial system, and to what extent have past reforms ameliorated financial repression? (3) What has been the impact of financial repression and development in China on economic growth? And (4) what needs to be done to develop the financial sector so that long-term growth in China may be sustained?

4.1. Why Repress the Financial System?

Why has China protected the monopoly of state-owned commercial banks by limiting the entry of domestic and foreign private banks, controlled interest rates, imposed relatively high reserve requirements, restricted the development debt and equity markets, and imposed strict controls on capital flows?[1] The reason is presumably the same as in other countries that pursued a similar heavy-industry-oriented development strategy and resorted to these same measures in varying degrees—because measures that repress the financial system maximize the flow of financial resources to government that it needs to implement its industrialization strategy.[2]

By maintaining the monopoly of state-owned banks, the government ensured that the bulk of the country's financial savings flowed by fiat to state-owned industrial enterprises. Restrictions on entry into the market of domestic and foreign private banks were obviously necessary to ensure the monopoly of state-owned banks. Because of their mandate to lend to the relatively unprofitable state-owned enterprises, state-owned banks would hardly have been in a position to compete for deposits with banks that were free to lend and attract deposits on a commercial basis. Similarly, restrictions on the development of debt and equity markets were necessary to ensure the predominance of state-owned banks and avoid a major diversion of financial savings to the nonstate sector.

By imposing ceilings on bank lending rates, the government ensures that the relatively unprofitable state-owned industrial enterprises have access to cheap credit. Ceilings on

[1] These are the main elements of a strategy financial repression. For a good overview, see Beim and Calomiris 2001.

[2] On the political economy of financial repression, see Denizer, Desai, and Gueorguiev 1998. David Li (2001, 3) provides a different rationale for financial repression in China: "Maintaining a mild financial repression in the reform era has been a very purposeful policy. The main intention has been to rely on the state monopoly of the financial sector to maintain macroeconomic stability for reform." Li's argument is examined more closely below.

lending rates lead naturally to an excess demand for credit, which means that nonpreferred borrowers have to pay very high interest rates or, as is more commonly the case, are simply rationed out of the market. Of course ceilings on lending rates lead naturally to ceilings on deposit rates, since the profitability of the state-owned banks must also be ensured, or at a minimum the banks' cost of intermediation must be covered. Interest rate ceilings, therefore, constitute an implicit tax on savers and nonpreferred investors and as such have deleterious effects on growth.

The reserves that commercial banks are required to hold in the central bank constitute a direct loan to the government, often at zero or low interest rates. Indeed required reserves are more in the nature of a transfer than a loan, since in practice the government is never obliged to repay, but instead obtains these resources as seignorage from its monopoly over the money supply. Reserve requirements may, however, be reasonable and prudential, since they facilitate clearing among banks and provide a precaution against financial crises in the event of heavy withdrawals of deposits. Often it is the case, however, that the required reserve ratio is set excessively high and the interest earned on reserves in the central bank is excessively low, which imposes a financial burden on commercial banks that is passed on to depositors in the form of lower deposit interest rates and higher lending rates (or smaller lending quotas), thus constituting another implicit tax on saving and investing.

Capital controls are another means of ensuring that resources flow where the government wants them to flow, principally the state-owned industrial sector. Capital controls also allow the government to avoid having to compete with foreign borrowers for the nation's financial saving, though such controls are not always effective, as we argued in the previous chapter was the case in China in the 1990s. Of course there are sound reasons for restricting capital flows in economies that have underdeveloped financial systems and weak financial regulations and supervision, since unless the financial system is reasonably well developed and financial regulations and supervision are in place, free capital mobility can (and too often has) led to banking and exchange rate crises (Prasad et al. 2003). Countries practicing financial repression, by definition, have underdeveloped financial systems, and because a large part of the banking sector is usually owned by the government, banking regulation and supervision is often neglected. Thus, necessity becomes a virtue—capital controls are a necessary component of financial repression, and repressed financial systems need capital controls to avoid financial crises.

The reinforcing nature of financial repression is an important feature of the regime and helps to explain why financial liberalization is economically and politically difficult.[3] When the government mandates that state-owned banks lend at artificially low interest rates to state-owned enterprises, even when they are not creditworthy, it is little wonder that the state-owned banks end up with a large stock of nonperforming loans. In effect, financial repression is a mechanism for transferring the losses of state-owned enterprises from the government's budget to the banking sector, which in turn passes the cost of financing the losses of state-owned enterprises on to depositors (in the form of lower deposit interest rates) and nonpreferred borrowers (in the form of higher lending rates and lower loan quotas). Once the state-owned banks become saddled with a large stock of nonperforming loans to state-owned enterprises, the government is faced with the dilemma of either maintaining the financial system as it is, with all its manifest inefficiencies, or abandoning its fundamental strategy and with it the state-owned enterprises. Repairing a repressed financial system, therefore, necessarily involves more than changing financial policy. It requires nothing less than a fundamental reorientation of development strategy, which inevitably entails heavy economic, political, and social costs.

---

[3] Li (2001, 6) refers to the "trap of financial repression," arguing that "once being implemented for years, the policy of financial repression gains a life of its own and is self-propelling."

4.2. How Repressed Is China's Financial System?

China is a classic case of a financially repressed economy, but everything is a matter of degree. To what extent is China's financial system repressed, and to what extent have past financial reforms ameliorated financial repression in China? A number of indicators of financial repression are featured in the literature, including the following (Beim and Calomiris 2001):

- Financial depth: The ratio of M2 to GDP.
- Bank lending: The ratio of commercial bank assets to commercial bank plus central bank assets.
- Private borrowing: The ratio of credit extended to the private sector to GDP.
- Reserve ratio: The ratio of bank reserves to deposits.
- Real interest rate: Nominal interest rate minus the inflation rate.
- Market value: The ratio of stock market capitalization to GDP.
- Bond market development: The ratio of government and corporate bond issuance to GDP.

Financial depth. The ratio of liquid liabilities of the financial system (measured by M2) to GDP is a commonly used measure of financial depth. As figure 4.1 indicates, by this measure, financial repression in China has rapidly diminished since 1980, the ratio M2 (M1 plus quasi money) to GDP increasing from about 33 percent in 1978 to almost 190 percent in 2004. It is apparent that the two main factors behind the growth of liquidity are (1) the monetization of economic activity (as indicated by the growth of M1 = currency in circulation plus demand deposits) and (2) the rapid increase in savings deposits, the main component of quasi money, which reached 115 percent of GDP in 2004.

The ratio of M2 to GDP at almost 190 percent in 2004 puts China ahead of just about every country in the world in terms of "financial depth." This fact alone indicates that, as a measure of financial development, the M2/GDP ratio is misleading. The ratio is exceptionally high in the case of China

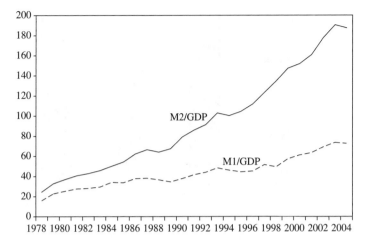

Figure 4.1. M1 and M2 as Percentage of GDP, 1978–2004. Source: *China Statistical Yearbook* 2005.

precisely because the strategy of financial repression has allowed few alternative nonmonetary saving instruments to develop. In addition, because households and businesses, other than state-owned enterprises, have only limited access to credit, they face a cash-in-advance constraint that requires them to accumulate relatively large saving deposit balances in anticipation of future expenditures and investments (Boyreau-Debray, undated). Hence the high M2/GDP ratio in China, while commonly interpreted as a leading indicator of financial development, also reflects the presence of financial repression in China's financial system.

Bank lending. Commercial bank credit as a share of total credit (including central bank credit) is used to measure the extent to which the nation's saving is allocated by the market (commercial banks) versus by the central bank. Before the reform process began in 1979, all credit was provided by the central bank, the People's Bank of China (PBOC). Between 1979 and 1985 the four major state-owned commercial banks were reestablished, each with an assigned sector of specializa-

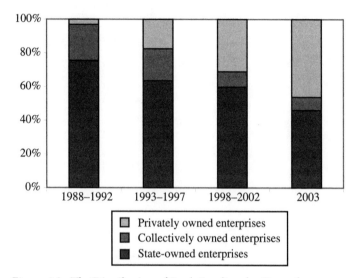

Figure 4.2. The Distribution of Bank Lending, by Type of Ownership of Borrower, 1988–2003. Source: *China Statistical Yearbook* 2005.

tion (agriculture, industry, construction, and foreign exchange). By the end of the 1980s, however, the system was loosened to allow the banks to operate across sectors. Thus, already by 1985, the ratio of commercial bank credit to total credit was 94 percent and by 2004 stood at 98 percent. The main weakness of this measure as an indicator of financial repression and development is that, in China's case, the bulk of commercial bank assets and liabilities is held by four big state-owned commercial banks, which are closely supervised and controlled by the central bank.

Private borrowing. A better measure of the commercialization of banking is provided by the share of credit extended to the private sector, which in China is exceptionally low, although it has increased significantly in recent years (as discussed in chapter 3). As figure 4.2 indicates, the private sector has gained limited access to bank loans only since the middle

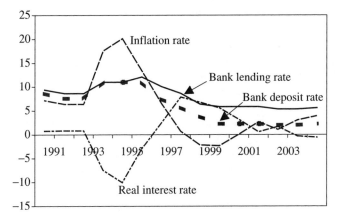

Figure 4.3. Bank Deposit and Lending Rates, 1990–2004 (percentages). Source: IMF, *International Financial Statistics*, 2004 Yearbook and September 2005.

to late 1990s. State enterprises still absorb a disproportionate share of bank loans relative to their contribution to output and employment, though their share in bank lending is gradually diminishing. Even at 33 percent, the private sector's share of bank loans in China is far below that of most developing countries (Boyreau-Debray, undated).

Interest rate ceilings.[4] Interest rate controls have become an important instrument of macroeconomic policy in China. In 1979, interest rates were restored to their pre–Cultural Revolution levels and then were successively increased during the 1980s (Lin, Cai, and Li 2003, 176). In 1988, the government adopted a policy of tying interest rates to the rate of inflation. As a result, since 1990 real interest rates have been positive in most years, 1994 and 1995, when inflation soared, being the main exceptions. Since the mid-1990s, as figure 4.3 indicates, interest rates have been successively lowered, along with the inflation rate. The first tentative step toward decontrolling

---

[4] In this section we examine only commercial bank interest rates, although interest rates on corporate bonds are also controlled.

interest rates was taken on October 24, 2004, when the government abolished the ceiling on lending rates, raising hopes and expectations that this move would mark the beginning of a long-awaited liberalization of interest rates.

The fact that real interest rates have generally been positive has led Li (2001, 3) to characterize China's financial system as one of "mild financial repression." What is critical in assessing the degree of financial repression is not, however, whether real interest rates have been positive or negative, but instead whether they reasonably reflect the opportunity cost of capital in the economy. By this criterion, financial repression in China can hardly be characterized as "mild," since the average real rate of return on investment, conservatively estimated in the previous chapter at about 20 percent, is four times the average real lending rate and 10 times the average real deposit rate.

Financial repression is reflected not only in the vast divergence between the return to depositors and the opportunity cost of capital, but also in the spread between lending and deposit interest rates. Lending rates must of course exceed deposit rates in order for banks to cover the costs of intermediation, holding required reserves, and carrying nonperforming loans on their balance sheets. The required reserve ratio in China (discussed in the next section) is not particularly onerous, but bank operating costs and the ratio of nonperforming loans are exceptionally high. Because of interest rate ceilings, China's banks are forced to compete with each other for deposits by establishing an extensive network of branches throughout the country. As a result, operating costs per bank in China are estimated to be almost four times higher, on average, than in other developing counties (Allen, Qian, and Qian 2005). Moreover, the ratio of nonperforming loans to total credit, at somewhere between 25 and 40 percent, itself requires a spread between deposit and lending rates of 33 to 66 percent.[5]

---

[5] This can be seen from the break-even condition for commercial banks, $r_D = r_L \left(1 - \dfrac{RR}{D} - \dfrac{NPL}{D} \right) - \dfrac{C}{D}$, where r_D is the deposit rate, r_L is the loan rate, RR is required reserves, NPL is the stock of nonperforming loans, C is the cost of intermediation, and D is the stock of deposits in the banking system.

TABLE 4.1
Reserve Requirement Rate (percentage of deposits)

	Rate on Rural Deposits	Rate on Urban Deposits	Unified Rate
1984	25	40	
1985–86			10
1987			12
1988–98			13
1998			8
1999			6
2003			7
2004			7.5

Source: Quarterly Report of People's Bank of China, summarized by China Economic Information Network: www.cei .gov.cn.

Reserve requirements. As mentioned above, while reserve requirements provide financing for the government, facilitate bank clearing, and serve as a precaution against heavy withdrawals of deposits, they also impose a financial burden—which in financially repressed economies is often excessive—on the banking system. As table 4.1 indicates, reserve requirements in China, until recently, were extremely high. In addition, prior to 1998, required reserves were not eligible for payments-clearing purposes, which required commercial banks to hold an additional 5 to 7 percent of deposits with the central bank for that purpose. In 1998, the reserve requirement ratio was reduced by about half, and the requirement of a clearing account at the central bank was abolished, significantly reducing the burden on commercial banks.

While the reserve requirement ratio has been coming down in China, the interest rate paid by the central bank on commercial bank required reserves has also been falling in absolute terms and relative to the interest rate commercial banks earn on long-term loans. As table 4.2 indicates, the return to commercial banks on required reserves is less than one-third what they earn on their long-term commercial loans. The in-

TABLE 4.2
Interest Rates on Long-Term Deposits and Loans and on Required Reserves,
Selected Dates, 1990–2005 (percentages)

	Rate on Long-Term Deposits (1)	Rate on Long-Term Loans (2)	Rate on Required Reserves (3)	Ratio of (3) to (2) (4)
August 21, 1990	11.52	11.16	n/a	
April 21, 1991	9.0	9.54	6.12	0.6
May 15, 1993	12.06	12.06	7.56	0.6
July 11, 1993	13.86	13.86	9.18	0.7
January 1, 1995	13.86	14.58	9.18	0.6
July 1, 1995	13.86	15.12	9.18	0.6
August 23, 1996	12.06	14.94	8.82	0.6
October 23, 1997	6.66	9.9	7.56	0.8
March 25, 1998	6.66	9.72	5.22	0.5
July 1, 1998	5.22	7.65	3.51	0.5
December 7, 1998	4.5	7.2	3.24	0.5
June 10, 1999	2.88	6.03	2.07	0.3
February 21, 2002	2.79	5.58	1.89	0.3
December 21, 2003	2.79	5.58	1.89	0.3
October 29, 2004	3.60	5.85	1.89	0.3
March 16, 2005	3.60	5.85	0.99	0.2

Source: China Statistical Yearbook, various issues.

terest rate on required reserves is even lower than what commercial banks pay to attract long-term deposits (2.8 percent
in 2002) or on average for long- and short-term deposits (2
percent in 2002). Reserve requirements in China, therefore,
constitute a significant burden on the banking system that of
course is passed along as an implicit tax on bank deposits
and loans.

Stock market capitalization. Stock markets are an important component of a well-developed financial system. Stock
markets mobilize saving, allocate investment, and play an important role in corporate governance. The standard measure
of stock market development is the ratio of market capital-

TABLE 4.3
Capital Raised and Market Capitalization in China's Stock Markets (100 million yuan)

	Shares Issued (100 m. shares)	Capital Raised (100 m. yuan)	Market Capitalization		Capitalization/GDP		Capital Raised/ GDFI (%)
			Total (100 m. yuan)	Negotiable (100 m. yuan)	Total (%)	Negotiable (%)	
1991	5	5	n/a	n/a			0.1
1992	21	95	n/a	n/a			1.1
1993	96	175	3,531	862	10.2	2.5	1.4
1994	91	327	3,691	969	7.9	2.1	1.9
1995	32	150	3,474	938	5.1	1.3	0.7
1996	86	415	9,842	2,867	14.5	4.2	1.8
1997	268	1,294	17,529	5,204	23.5	6.9	5.1
1998	106	842	19,506	5,746	24.9	7.3	3.0
1999	123	945	26,471	8,214	32.2	10.0	3.2
2000	512	2,103	48,091	16,088	53.7	17.9	6.4
2001	141	1,252	43,522	14,463	45.3	15.0	3.4
2002	292	962	38,329	12,485	36.5	11.9	2.3
2003	281	1,358	42,458	13,179	36.2	11.7	2.6
2004	227	1,511	37,056	11,689	27.1	8.5	2.4

Source: *China Statistical Yearbook*, various issues.

ization to GDP. By this measure, as table 4.3 indicates, stock markets in China (in Shanghai and Shenzhen) have developed rapidly since they were first established in 1991.

A number of unique features of China's stock markets need to be considered, however, in evaluating the role of stock markets in financial development. One of the most important is that only about a third of publicly issued shares are freely traded. The other two-thirds are held by the state and through cross-holdings by state-owned enterprises and by law cannot be traded on the stock exchanges.

The market capitalization to GDP for all shares reached a high of 54 percent in 2000, a ratio roughly comparable to those of Japan and Korea. However, in terms of tradable shares, the market capitalization ratio reached only 18 percent in 2000, which is far below the ratios in most other Asian countries (Green 2003). Since 2000, share prices and the market capitalization ratio have fallen significantly.

In spite of its rapid growth, China's stock markets have made only a modest contribution to mobilizing savings and financing investment. As table 4.3 indicates, capital raised in China's stock markets amounts to but a small fraction of total fixed investment (GDFI). Even for publicly traded companies, the share of capital raised in the stock market is quite small (Allen, Qian, and Qian 2005).

The other important role of the stock market is to exercise corporate governance. When shareholding is diffused among many small individual shareholders, corporate governance is performed mainly through the corporate takeover mechanism and thus requires a rather deep and highly liquid market to be effective, which of course does not characterize China's stock markets, where two-thirds of outstanding shares are nontradable. When shareholding is concentrated, as it is in China with about two-thirds of issued shares in the hands of the government and government-owned enterprises, corporate governance is exercised from within the firm rather than through the market for corporate control. The problem with this mechanism of corporate governance in China's case, however, is that the majority shareholder and the management of most of China's listed companies are one and the same, the government. Not surprisingly, therefore, most studies find that there has been little improvement in economic performance of companies after becoming publicly traded. Indeed, about 13 percent of publicly listed companies, having performed profitably for at least three years prior to being listed (a condition for being listed), subsequently were running losses in 2002 (Green 2003).

Bond market development. The literature on finance and growth gives little attention to the role of bond markets, but clearly they are an important component of a well-developed financial system. As table 4.4 indicates, the stock of outstand-

TABLE 4.4
Bonds Outstanding by Type and as Percentage of GDP (RMB 100 million)

	Treasury Bond	Policy Financial Bond	Corporate Bond	Total	Total/GDP (%)
1991	1,060		331	1,391	6.6
1992	1,283		822	2,105	7.9
1993	1,541		802	2,343	6.5
1994	2,286	776	682	2,976	6.3
1995	3,300	1,613	647	5,560	9.5
1996	4,361	2,400	598	7,359	10.8
1997	5,509	3,487	521	9,517	12.7
1998	7,766	5,121	677	13,564	17.3
1999	10,542	6,447	779	17,768	21.6
2000	13,020	7,383	862	21,265	23.8
2001	15,618	8,534	1,009	25,161	26.2
2002	19,336	10,054	1,070	30,460	29.1
2003	22,604	11,650	1,136	35,390	26.2
2004	25,778	14,019	1,233	41,030	29.1

Source: *Almanac of China's Finance and Banking Statistics* 2002; *China Statistical Yearbook* 2003; Gao 1999; and CEIC.

ing bonds has increased rapidly in China since the early 1990s. The main issuer of bonds in China is the Ministry of Finance (MOF), which because of the growth of fiscal deficits and a law, since 1995, that forbids the monetization of government deficits, the central government has had to resort increasingly to debt finance. Even more rapid is the growth of "policy bonds," which are issued mainly by the China Development Bank (CDB) and used primarily to mobilize long-term financing for infrastructure investments. The corporate bond market, as table 4.4 indicates, is still very much in its infancy.

In China, treasury and policy bonds are placed mainly with commercial banks and priced using various auction pricing methods.[6] The trading of treasury and policy bonds is re-

[6] The China Development Bank introduced further market innovations with the issuance of callable and putable bonds, asymmetric bonds, subdebt, reopening bonds, and STRIPS.

stricted to the interbank market.[7] As such, the interbank market functions as a source of long-term financing and as a mechanism for banks to adjust their asset liquidity, rather than as a money market, the typical case in more financially developed countries. The issuance of corporate bonds is subject to strict administrative control, and is confined to state-owned enterprises undertaking projects of "national significance." Furthermore, the interest rate on corporate bonds is administratively determined.

Financial Repression and Development Overall

It is impossible to add up all of these disparate measures into a single index of financial repression and development. It is apparent nonetheless that each of the indicators summarized here has shown some, albeit limited, improvement since the early 1990s. The most impressive development is the increase in financial depth (indicted by the rise in the ratio of M2/GDP), but as we have argued, this development is in part due to the lack of alternative saving instruments and, given the cash-in-advance constraints, the limited access households and most businesses have to bank credit. In recent years, access to credit by households and non-state-owned enterprises has improved, but only to a limited extent. Stock and bond markets have developed, but they are still heavily regulated and controlled by the government. Thus, it must be concluded that in spite of some positive developments, the financial system in China is still very repressed.

4.3. FINANCE AND GROWTH IN CHINA

For a long time the role of the financial sector in economic development was debated. At the heart of this debate was the question of whether growth causes financial development or

---

[7] The interbank market appeared in June 1997 as an alternative solution for the banks to trade their bond holdings after being banned from trading on stock exchanges.

financial development causes growth. In the meantime, a lot of theoretical and empirical work has been carried out to resolve this issue, much of it conveniently summarized in a recent paper by Levine (2003). The theoretical work clearly shows that financial instruments, markets, and institutions arise to mitigate the effects of information and transaction costs and in the process have a beneficial impact on saving rates, investment decisions, technological innovation, and growth rates (Levine 2003, 2). Three general conclusions emerge from the empirical studies on the link between financial development and growth according to Levine (2003, 3): "(1) countries with better functioning banks and markets grow faster, but the degree to which a country is bank-based or market-based does not matter much, (2) simultaneity bias does not seem to drive this conclusion, and (3) better functioning financial systems ease the external financing constraints that impede firm and industrial expansion, suggesting that this is one channel through which financial development matters for growth."

Many of the empirical studies of the financial development–growth nexus use cross-country panel-data methodology to estimate a growth equation in which financial development variables appear along with the traditional growth determinants (e.g., the investment rate, employment growth, human capital accumulation, and assorted other variables featured in the empirical growth literature and reviewed in chapter 2 above). This approach has been replicated in a number of studies of the financial development–growth nexus in China, using cross-provincial panel data in place of cross-country panel data.

The remarkable finding of most of these studies is that the relationships between financial development and growth that emerge from the cross-country data are absent in, indeed are contradicted by, the cross-provincial data for China. Thus, while across countries higher levels of financial development are associated with higher rates of growth, across Chinese provinces, higher rates of financial development, particularly in the banking sector, are associated with lower rates of provincial growth (Boyreau-Debray, undated). While cross-country studies find that financial development reduces income inequality among countries (Greenwood and Jovanovic 1990; Clarke, Xu, and Zou 2003), across Chinese provinces financial development is associated with increased inter-provincial income disparity (Qi et al. 2003). While there is a large empirical literature showing that the more developed a country's legal system, the more efficient its financial system and the higher its rate of growth (La Porta et al. 1998; Levine 1998), across Chinese provinces it has been found that "an enhanced legal system does not have a significant effect on the average (provincial) growth rate" and "has no effect on financial depth" (Lu and Yao 2003). Another recent study (Allen, Qian, and Qian 2005, 57) purports to demonstrate that "China is a significant counterexample to the findings of the existing literature on law, finance and growth," arguing that informal financing mechanisms "can substitute for and do better than standard channels and mechanisms."

These studies, taken at face value, would seem to challenge the central thesis of this study, namely that financial sector development is crucial for China to be able to sustain growth in the future. It is useful therefore to look more closely at their results and interpretations. The consistency of these results would suggest that at a technical level the empirical findings are valid, and indeed we accept them as such. What we take issue with, however, is their interpretation. Indeed, we argue that these results can be easily reconciled with, and indeed support, the thesis put forward in this study, that financial sector development is crucial for sustaining China's growth.

Financial development and growth in China. A necessary condition for using cross-provincial data to test the financial development–growth nexus is a low degree of capital mobility among provinces. Boyreau-Debray (undated) tests for this condition using the Feldstein-Horioka test of capital mobility, the null hypothesis of which is that with perfect capital mobility there should be no significant correlation between saving and investment rates across provinces. Boyreau-Debray finds a highly significant correlation between saving and investment rates across provinces, from which she concludes that there is a low degree of capital mobility between Chinese provinces.[8] There is also significant disparity in the development of banking among provinces (as measured by the ratio of deposits to provincial GDP), but there is no statistically significant relation between this measure of provincial financial depth and the rate of provincial growth.

On the face of it, this result would appear to contradict the conventional view, but Boyreau-Debray reveals that financial depth is not positively related to provincial growth because the bulk of bank credit is allocated to relatively inefficient state-owned enterprises. This result does not, therefore, suggest that China should not pursue financial development, but rather that as long as the financial system is dominated by state-owned banks that lend mainly to inefficient state-owned enterprises, expansion of the banking system has only a weak, or possibly no, effect on economic growth. As such, these results are an indictment of the status quo and a powerful argument for financial liberalization.

Financial development and regional inequality. The empirical finding, also based on panel data for Chinese provinces over the period 1978–98, that financial development (measured by the ratio of bank loans to provincial GDP) "contributes to the enlargement of urban-rural income disparity" likewise derives from the fact that most bank loans go to relatively inefficient state-owned enterprises (Qi et al. 2003). Increasing levels of financial depth at the provincial level exacerbated regional income inequality, as the authors of this study note, "because more funds were directed by government to meet the financial demands of large SOEs" (6). As a result, they argue, "farmers and town-and-village enterprises were more financially constrained," to the detriment of rural-urban income equality. Moreover, the authors show that this bias in-

---

[8] Most studies of intraregional capital mobility for most other countries find no statistically significant correlation between saving and investment across provinces, confirming the null hypothesis. China is therefore an exception, and hence the cross-country methodology can be applied to study finance and growth across Chinese provinces.

tensified in the 1990s, as the government relied more on the banking sector and less on direct government subsidies to finance investment and cover the losses of state-owned enterprises. Again, these results argue strongly for increased financial sector development to improve the functioning of bank credit allocation and to provide alternative financing mechanisms through the development of corporate bond and securities markets.

Legal reform, financial development, and growth. Lu and Yao (2003) develop an index of "the effectiveness of the legal system" at the provincial level, and enter this variable into a regression equation for economic growth along with variables for financial development and other growth determinants. As a measure of the effectiveness of the provincial legal system, the authors use the number of court cases closed in each year as a ratio of the total number of cases taken up by the court in the same year. Their results show that the more effective is the legal system of a province, the larger the share of credit allocated to the private sector, but the lower the share of private investment. The positive effect of legal reform on financial development and the negative effect on private investment offset each other, such that no statistically significant relationship is found between effectiveness of the legal system and economic growth across provinces.

The explanation provided by the authors for the negative relationship between the effectiveness of the legal system and the share of credit to the private sector is that where the legal system is weak, financial resources are more easily channeled, through both legal and illegal means, from state-owned enterprises to private ones. Thus, it is argued that as long as China's financial system remains repressed, improvements in the legal system will reduce the flow of finance to the nation's more efficient private enterprises and therefore reduce growth. Taking these results at face value, the obvious and compelling policy conclusion is simultaneously to improve the legal system and eliminate financial repression.

The relative efficiency of informal finance. It has been argued that China provides a "significant counterexample to the findings of the existing literature on law, finance and growth" (Allen, Qian, and Qian, 2005). None of the studies summarized above supports this claim, but Allen, Qian, and Qian (2005) assert it nonetheless on the grounds that the "informal sector," which they dubiously define as all firms other than state-owned and publicly traded firms, grew much faster than the formal sector (state-owned enterprises) in spite of having weak legal protection and limited access to formal finance. They conclude that in China "there exist very effective, nonstandard financing channels and corporate governance mechanisms to support the growth of the informal sector" (1). They assert that "these informal channels and mechanisms are based on reputation and relationships, and they can substitute for and do better than standard channels and mechanisms" (1). The evidence they provide, however, is purely anecdotal.

There is no doubt that non-state-owned enterprises have only limited access to the formal financial system (i.e., banks) and yet have grown far more rapidly than state-owned enterprises. This does not, however, constitute evidence that informal financial channels and mechanisms work better than formal ones. It simply reveals that nonstate enterprises were able to find alternative sources of financing, at whatever cost.[9] In the 1980s, it was collectively owned township and village enterprises—not private companies—that spurred industrial growth. They succeeded in the 1980s, where private companies did not, mainly because fiscal decentralization in the 1980s empowered subnational governments to engage in entrepreneurship to maximize their revenues, for example by investing in township and village enterprises. Private companies only became important in the 1990s, after they gained formal legal status that allowed them to attract foreign investment and get increased, albeit still limited, access to the

[9] It is reported that the curb market rate of interest in China is 50 to 100 percent higher than official rates (Garnaut et al. 2000).

banking system. The evidence suggests that informal financial channels work, but not that they necessarily work better than well-developed formal ones. If financial development leads to the displacement of informal financial channels, that is presumably because the formal ones work better. If not, then the thesis put forward by Allen, Qian, and Qian (2005) must be judged valid. The market will decide this issue, but in order for that to happen the market has to be free to work—in other words, the formal financial system must be liberalized and developed.

4.4. Strategy of Financial Development

Economic theory and empirical evidence argue that financial development is an important determinant of long-term growth. The empirical studies of financial development and growth in China, reviewed in the previous section, by our interpretation strongly support the general view as applicable to the case of China. The question is how China should go about developing its financial sector. Should it put priority on reforming the banking sector, should it focus instead on developing the stock and bond markets, or is it more desirable to undertake simultaneously banking sector reform and financial market development?

On the question of which is the better, a bank-based or a market-based financial system, there has been much debate. Those who argue in favor of a bank-based system do so by pointing out the comparative shortcomings of a market-based system (Levine 2003, 22). Some argue that banks are better able, and have stronger incentives, to collect information about firms' prospects and hence do a better job of allocating investment than a stock market. It is also maintained that banks, through the long-term relationship they establish with their clients, are in a better position to exercise corporate governance than stock markets that rely on the market for corporate control. Concentrated ownership of stocks can improve the functioning of corporate governance, but problems from concentrated ownership can also arise when majority owners use their control to benefit themselves at the expense of the firm and its minority shareholders.

On the other hand, bank-based systems have shortcomings as well. Banks, as issuers of debt, are likely to be more risk-averse than stock markets, perhaps reducing innovation and growth. Banks may also become so deeply involved in the business of their clients that they become unable to exercise arm's-length corporate governance. It is also argued that financial markets "provide a richer set of risk management tools that permit greater customization of risk ameliorating instruments" (Levine 2003, 28).

Finally, there are those who argue that the question of which is better, a bank-based or market-based system, is unimportant. Banks and markets may be better regarded as complements rather than substitutes. For example, Levine (2003, 29) points out that "by spurring competition for corporate control and by offering alternative means of financing investment, securities markets may reduce the potentially harmful effects of excessive bank power." Indeed, there is empirical evidence that stock market development increases the use of bank finance in developing countries (Demirguc-Kunt and Maksimovic 1996).

The question of which system is better is essentially an empirical one. From his survey of the evidence, Levine (2003, 69) concludes that "after controlling for overall financial development, cross-country comparisons do not suggest that distinguishing between bank-based and market-based financial systems is a first-order concern in understanding the process of economic growth." It is almost always the case that developing countries with underdeveloped financial systems are bank-based, but as they grow, financial markets become relatively more important. The empirical evidence suggests, therefore, that the preferable strategy for financial development is one that allows both banks and markets to flourish without tilting the balance in favor of one or the other.

This is essentially the strategy we recommend for China.[10] China cannot afford to ignore the inefficiency of financial intermediation in the banking sector. Nor should it forego the advantages that can come from the development of efficient bond and stock markets. The devil, as always, is in the details, and many detailed questions need to be addressed in order make the implementation of such a strategy of financial sector development effective. In the three following chapters we attempt to answer some of those questions by examining banking sector reform (chapter 5), developments in the bond market (chapter 6), and the rise and fall of the stock market (chapter 7). In the final chapter (chapter 8) we examine the conduct of macroeconomic policy and performance in China's financially repressed economy.

[10] The case for this strategy has been made by Chen Yuan, governor of the China Development Bank, who argues, "Long-term sustainable economic growth requires the development of a sound and efficient financial system that accommodates the coordinated development of three forms of finance—budgetary finance, bank finance and securities finance" (Chen 2003, 2).

CHAPTER 5

Banking Sector Reform

CHINA HAS A large, yet fundamentally repressed, financial system, dominated by a weak and inefficient banking sector. As we argued in the previous chapter, the disproportionate size of the banking sector is a manifestation of financial repression, just as is its weakness and fragility. If China is to succeed in its efforts to liberalize the financial system, one can expect not only a major restructuring of the banking sector, but also a scaling down of its size, in relative if not absolute terms, and a significant increase in the role of securities markets in the financial system.

In this chapter we examine the manifestations of China's oversized and underperforming banking sector and what measures are being taken to redress the problem. In subsequent chapters we examine the problems in China's financial markets and find that China's mammoth, state-dominated commercial banks are an obstacle not only to efficient intermediation in the banking sector, but also to the development of the bond market and the functioning of the stock markets.

5.1. KEY FEATURES OF THE BANKING SECTOR

The most remarkable thing about China's financial system is that in just 20 years it has grown from practically nothing to a size, relative to GDP, comparable to that of the United States. As table 5.1 indicates, the ratio of financial assets to GDP in China in 2004 was 230 percent, slightly higher than for the United States (229 percent). Fueling the growth of the financial system was, as we have already explained in earlier chapters, China's rapid growth and structural change, the

TABLE 5.1
The Size and Structure of the Financial System in China and in the United States
in 2004 (percentages)

	China		United States	
	Share in Total Assets	% of GDP	Share in Total Assets	% of GDP
Bank loans	72	165	26	59
Equities	12	26	45	103
Government bonds	16	38	18	41
Corporate bonds	<1	<1	11	25
Total	100	230	100	229

Source: *China Almanac of Banking and Financial Statistics* 2004; Barth, Koepp and Zhou 2004; CEIC.

monetization of the economy, and a high and rising household saving rate, which together led to an extraordinary expansion in demand for financial assets.

The legacy of central planning and government policies that inhibited the development of securities markets has essentially limited the supply of financial assets to bank deposits. As table 5.1 indicates, bank loans outstanding accounted for 72 percent of all financial assets and 165 percent of GDP in 2004. In the United States, by contrast, bank loans outstanding account for only 26 percent of financial assets and amount to only about 60 percent of GDP. As table 5.1 indicates, equity and bond markets in China have yet to play a significant role, much less to dominate the financial system as they do in the United States.

Another salient feature of the banking sector in China is the dominant role of government. State-owned commercial banks, together with joint-stock and joint-venture banks in which the government owns a large, if not majority, share account for the bulk of bank deposits. Not surprisingly, the government has used its near monopoly in the banking sector to lend mostly to itself—that is, to state-owned and controlled enterprises and to the government directly. As table 5.2 shows, the private business sector (a significant but not exclusive part of "other" in

TABLE 5.2
Deposits and Loans by Ownership in 2004 (percentages)

Deposit Institution Receiving	Share in Total Deposits	Recipient of Loan	Share in Total Loans
State-owned commercial bank	59	SOE	48
State-owned policy bank	2	Agriculture	10
Other commercial bank	22	Consumer	10
Rural & urban credit co-op	12	Government	8
Other	6	Other	24
Total	100	Total	100

Source: Anderson 2005d.

table 5.2) accounts for but a small share of loans, an issue that was highlighted in previous chapters.

5.2. PROBLEMS OF THE BANKING SECTOR

These two features of China's financial system—a system dominated by the banking sector and a banking sector dominated by the government—lie at the heart of the problems that beset it. Before examining what government is doing to fix these problems, it is useful to summarize their main manifestations.

Nonperforming Loans

The most prominent and widely discussed manifestation of the weakness of China's government-dominated banking system is its stock of nonperforming loans (NPLs), which according to official estimates (for 2004) amounts to about $300 billion, or 15 percent of outstanding loans. Some independent analysts argue that the official estimate significantly understates the stock of NPLs, which (for 2004) may actually be as high as $500 billion, or 25 to 30 percent of loans outstanding, or about 50 percent of GDP (UBS 2005; Garcia-Herrero and

Santabarbara 2004).[1] At 25 percent, the NPL ratio for China is double that of the Philippines and Indonesia, which have the weakest and most crisis-prone banking sectors in Asia. Even the 25–30 percent NPL ratio understates the problem, since it does not take into account the stock of NPLs that have been transferred from the state-owned commercial banks to government-owned asset management companies (AMCs) since 1999, which amounts to another $200 billion in bad debt. Thus, in total the stock of bad loans may be as high as 40 to 50 percent of outstanding loans, or 60 to 70 percent of GDP.

While NPLs constitute a problem of major proportions, there are indications that government efforts to encourage better lending practices by state-owned banks and improve the performance of the state-owned enterprises that borrow from them are having a positive effect. As figures 5.1 and 5.2 indicate, both the stock and flow of NPLs are declining. In 1997, the stock of NPLs reached its all-time high as a result of a massive expansion in bank lending to SOEs in the early 1990s, during a period of rapid monetary expansion, accelerating inflation, and declining profitability of SOEs. Since 1999, according to both official and unofficial estimates, the NPL ratio has been declining. In part the decline in the stock of NPLs is due to the transfer of $200 billion worth of NPLs to the AMCs since 1999, but as figure 5.2 indicates, the NPL ratio has also been brought down by an improvement in the quality of new loans. This improvement, as shown by the decline in the ratio of the flow of NPLs to new loans, may be a reflection of both better lending practices on the part of state-owned banks and improved profitability of their traditional borrowers, the SOEs (an issue to which we return subsequently).

Capital Inadequacy

With an NPL ratio of about 25 percent, not surprisingly China's banking system is effectively insolvent. As figure 5.3 indicates, bank capital as a percentage of assets has fallen

---

[1] Official estimates understate the stock of NPLs for several reasons.

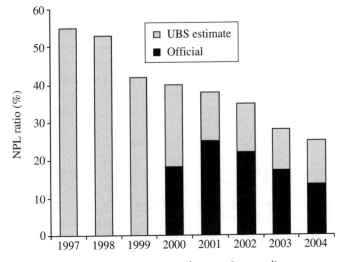

Figure 5.1. NPLs as a Percentage of Loans Outstanding, 1997–2004. Source: Anderson 2005d, 17.

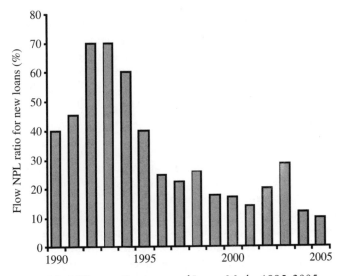

Figure 5.2. NPLs as a Percentage of Loans Made, 1995–2005. Source: Anderson 2005d, 17.

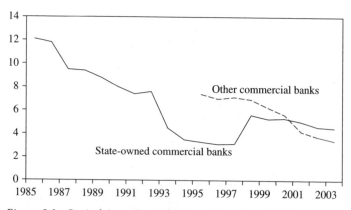

Figure 5.3. Capital Asset Ratio for State-Owned and Other Commercial Banks, 1985–2003 (percentages). Source: Lardy 1999; China Almanac of Finance and Banking 2004.

steadily since the mid-1980s, and currently stands at about 4 percent. The rise in the capital adequacy ratio in 1999 was the result of a RMB 270 billion capital infusion undertaken by the government, the first of a series of bank recapitalizations aimed at reducing the state-owned bank's NPL burden. Since the bad loans on the balance sheets of the banking system greatly exceed bank capital and loan loss reserves (about 1 to 2 percent of bank assets), the net worth of China's banks is negative to the tune of about $200 to 300 billion.

Profitability

In just about any other country, an insolvent banking system would trigger a financial or banking crisis, but not in China. One reason there has not been such a crisis is that although the banking sector is insolvent, it is not illiquid. Indeed, banks, in spite of their large stock of nonperforming loans, have continuously maintained a positive operating surplus. As figure 5.4 indicates, the government-set interest rate ceiling set on deposits and the interest rate floor on loans have been sufficient to ensure that even though the commercial

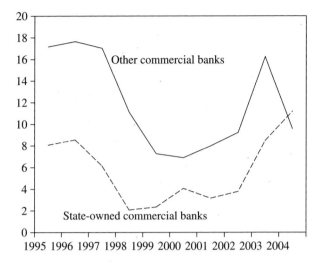
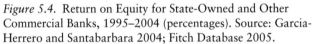

Figure 5.4. Return on Equity for State-Owned and Other Commercial Banks, 1995–2004 (percentages). Source: Garcia-Herrero and Santabarbara 2004; Fitch Database 2005.

banks earn interest on only about 75 percent of their loans, it is more than enough to cover the interest banks have to pay on 100 percent of their deposits.[2] Furthermore, even though operating costs are high, in particular the wage costs of maintaining an extensive network of branches, net interest earnings have been sufficient to keep China's commercial banks out of the red, as figures 5.4 and 5.5 indicate.

That the banking system is highly liquid and hence able to meet its interest obligations on deposits is an important source of confidence for depositors, but just as important is the perceived implicit guarantee that the government would in any event honor the liabilities of state-owned banks to its depositors. While the implicit government guarantee to bail out the banking system in the event of a crisis is reassuring to depositors and forestalls an immediate crisis, it also constitutes a

[2] Lending rates in China are about 3.5 times higher than deposit rates, which means that banks can be liquid with two-thirds of their loans nonperforming.

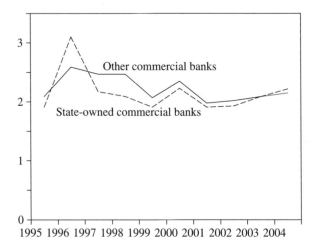

Figure 5.5. Net Interest Margin for State-Owned and Other Commercial Banks, 1995–2004 (percentages). Source: Garcia-Herrero and Santabarbara 2004; Fitch 2005.

fundamental source of the problem of the banking sector, since not only depositors, but lenders too perceive an implicit government guarantee, which creates moral hazard behavior on the part of the banks. The government therefore faces a dilemma: to remove the implicit guarantee might well trigger a banking crisis, but to maintain the guarantee to some extent undermines the government's efforts to encourage more prudent lending practices by the banks, an issue to which we return later.

Another source of protection for China's insolvent banking sector, and at the same time a source of weakness in the financial system, is the near monopoly position of state-owned banks. The state has imposed formal and informal restrictions that inhibit both domestic and foreign competition in the market for financial assets. Limitations on corporate equity and bond issuance, together with restrictions on international capital flows, ensure that the bulk of financial assets remain in the banking system. Moreover, restrictions on the scale and funding sources of both domestic and foreign non-state-owned banks mean that depositors have only limited alternatives to the large state-owned banks. Under current circumstances, there is, therefore, little likelihood of a significant withdrawal of deposits from the state-owned banks that dominate the system.

In the next section we examine the measures the government is taking to strengthen the banking sector and develop the financial system. As the foregoing discussion suggests, many of the measures that will be required may well have the effect of increasing the vulnerability of the banking sector in its current manifestation. It is important therefore to consider not only what needs to be done to develop the financial system, but also the proper timing and sequencing of reforms so as to avoid making the banking sector weaker at the same time the government is trying to make it stronger.

5.3. MEASURES TAKEN TO STRENGTHEN THE BANKING SECTOR

A number of measures need to be taken to strengthen the banking sector and develop the financial system. The immediate problem is the stock of NPLs that renders the banking sector insolvent. Eliminating the NPLs from the banks' balance sheets will not solve anything, however, if measures are not taken at the same time to change the banking practices that gave rise to the NPLs in the first place. Thus, a number of measures must be taken to change the management practices of the banks, important among them the incentive structure that guides bank managers. In addition to giving bank managers more skills and better incentives, market forces must be given more scope in determining the allocation of credit, which will require greater liberalization of interest rates than has occurred so far. In order to make credit markets work more efficiently the government must allow for much greater competition within the banking sector and between the banking sector and alternative suppliers of financial assets at home and abroad. To make the banking sector more competitive the government must consider privatizing state-owned banks, easing restrictions on the entry of domestic private and foreign-owned banks, developing bond and equity markets, and ultimately liberalizing the capital account. Since some of these measures work at cross-purposes, the implementation of these measures must follow a proper sequence to minimize the potential for disruptions in the financial system.

Resolving the NPL Problem

The government has taken two approaches to resolving banking sector NPLs. One has been to inject cash into the state-owned banks that they use to write off their NPLs. The first cash injection of RMB 270 billion ($33 billion) occurred in 1998 and was financed by a special issue of government bonds. A second cash injection ($45 billion) into two state-owned banks (Bank of China and China Construction Bank) occurred at the end of 2003 and was financed from foreign exchange reserves.[3]

The second approach was the establishment of four asset management companies (AMCs), each linked to one of the state-owned banks, to acquire NPLs from the state-owned banks. Between the end of 1999 and the end of 2000, the banks transferred about RMB 1.4 trillion ($170 billion) of NPLs that had been contracted before 1996 to the AMCs mainly in exchange for interest-earning bonds issued by the AMCs.[4] Thus, as of mid-2005, the state-owned banks had effectively disposed of about $250 billion in NPLs, either through recapitalization (cash injections) or by carving out NPLs from the banks' balance sheets. The approximately

[3] It has been suggested that the government chose BOC and CCB for recapitalization "because their superior performance would make it possible for earlier public listing" (Pei and Sharai 2004, 5). A third cash injection into the ICBC of $15 to 30 billion occurred in 2005.

[4] In addition, the banks got debt relief and cash transfers from the PBOC of about RMB 400 billion, the latter amount effectively constituting monetization of NPLs.

$300 billion in outstanding NPLs (as of 2005) discussed above is what remained after the recapitalizations and NPL carve-outs and what has been accumulated since.

From the banks' perspective, recapitalization and NPL carve-outs amount to about the same thing since the net effect on the banks' balance sheets is the same (Anderson 2005d). In the case of a carve-out, bad assets (NPLs) are exchanged for good, or at least better, assets (treasury bonds), with bank equity unchanged. In the case of recapitalization, the banks write off bad loans against equity and then the government restores equity with a cash injection. Both approaches lead to an equivalent reduction in NPLs and an increase in the banks' capital adequacy ratios.

From the viewpoint of government finance, however, the two approaches are quite different, as least in the near term. In the case of recapitalization, the bailout is financed currently either by the central bank issuing money (monetizing the bad debt) or by the finance ministry issuing bonds, and hence has implications for monetary and fiscal policy and overall macroeconomic balance. In the case of NPL carve-outs, the bad debt remains in the system, having simply been transferred from one government entity, the state-owned banks, to another, the AMCs. Since the liabilities of the AMCs, like the state-owned banks, carry an implicit government guarantee, the stock of NPLs carved out remains a contingent liability of the government to be financed sometime in the future either through monetization or issuing government debt when the AMCs bonds mature.[5] The macroeconomic implications of the NLP carve-outs depend, therefore, on how much of the bad debt can be recovered by the AMCs by direct collection and foreclosure from borrowers, resale of the NPLs to other entities, and debt-equity swaps. In China, evidence suggests that at best the AMCs will succeed in recovering only about 25 percent of the book value of the NPLs they

[5] Note that the government guarantee on AMC liabilities is not explicit, but it is widely recognized that without state backing of the AMCs, the carve-out achieves nothing, since without government guarantees the AMC bonds are no better than the bad loans they replaced.

hold, which means a contingent liability to the government of about $125 billion (Pei and Shirai 2004). The total contingent liability of the government to resolve the existing stock of NPLs held by the banks ($300 billion) and the AMCs ($170 billion) is therefore about $350 billion, assuming a recovery rate of 25 percent on both bank-held and AMC-held NPLs.

Not surprisingly, the question of whether the government can "afford" to bail out the banks and the implications of doing so for macroeconomic stability and medium-run growth has been widely debated. It has been suggested, for example, that the "greatest threat to the stability of China's financial markets is fiscal sustainability, and the biggest threat to fiscal sustainability is successive rounds of bank recapitalization" (Woo 2003, 24). Woo argues that China's expansionary fiscal policy, which he suggests is what has been keeping GDP growth high, will be put in jeopardy if the government issues substantial amounts of additional debt to finance bank recapitalization because the interest costs on increased government debt will require either a tax increase or a reduction of government expenditures, which would likely fall heaviest on government investment, and hence impact growth.

A more optimistic outlook is offered by UBS economist Jonathan Anderson (2005d). Of the total bailout cost of $350 billion (75 percent of the combined bank-held and AMC-held stock of NPLs), Anderson argues that the banks can afford to write down about $20 billion of NPLs annually out of loan loss provisions and pretax operating profits. Over five years, this amounts to about a $100 billion reduction in the fiscal cost of bailing out the banks. In addition, Anderson suggests that "the government could potentially raise as much as $40 billion through a combination of equity listings and private placements—funds that would be used to offset the costs of writing off NPLs" (2005d, 31). This would bring the cost of bailing out the state-owned banks down to $210 billion. If one adds in the cost of cleaning up and consolidating the rural credit cooperative and city banks, which Anderson puts at about $70 billion, the total cost comes to $280 billion, or 17 percent of 2004 GDP. If we assume the government borrowing rate is 5 percent, the annual financing cost would be less than 1 percent of GDP. The cost would be even lower if the government were to monetize at least part of the stock of NPLs, which it can accomplish without creating inflationary pressure since the demand for money in China will continue to expand rapidly with growth and structural change in the economy. Even the most optimistic assessment of the cost of bailing the banks out of their NPL problem rests on one crucial assumption, however, namely that banking practices can be changed so as to avoid an excessive accumulation of NPLs in the future.

Institutional Reform

Institutional reforms have been under way since the commercial banking system in China was established in the 1980s. In 1994 the government completed the process, begun in the early 1980s, of removing commercial banking activities from the PBOC and transferring them to state-owned commercial banks. At the same time, policy-lending activities of the four SOCBs were transferred to three newly established policy-lending banks: the China Development Bank, the Export Import Bank of China, and the Agriculture Development Bank of China. The early 1990s was a period of rapid credit expansion and was accompanied by a proliferation of new joint-stock and city commercial banks set up mainly by local governments.

Not surprisingly, when the state-owned banks were established, they were run very much like any other state-owned enterprise, with management appointed by the state with close oversight from the Party. In additional, regional and local governments played a decisive role in appointing managers of branches in their jurisdictions and intervened heavily in lending decisions. Bank regulation and supervision were dispersed among various departments of the PBOC, the China Banking Regulatory Commission (CBRC), and the Ministry of Finance and were ineffective in maintaining the integrity of the system. The result of poor banking practices and weak regulation was, of course, the accumulation of NPLs, which reached its peak in 1997 at more than 50 percent of outstanding loans.

In the wake of the Asian financial crisis and the massive accumulation of NPLs in the early and mid-1990s, the government has taken a number of wide-ranging measures to improve the management and practices of its state-owned banks. Among the measures taken include the corporatization of the state-owned banks, the centralization of personnel decisions, the introduction of international accounting standards, the separation of policy lending from commercial lending, and the strengthening of supervisory and regulatory functions under the China Bank Regulatory Commission (Anderson 2005d).

Everything is, of course, a matter of degree, and there is no question that as long as the banks remain in the hands of the state, the principal-agent problem will remain and moral hazard will continue to undermine good banking practices. However, there is also no question that the government has taken significant steps to improve the governance and operating procedures in the banking sector. As noted above, these measures appear already to be having a positive impact on the quality of bank lending.

Increasing Domestic Competition

In order for the institutional reforms in the state-owned banks to bear fruit, the level of competition that the banks face must be significantly increased. Increased competition can and should arise from three sources: domestic non-state-owned banks, foreign-owned banks, and the nonbank segments of the financial system, principally bond and equity markets.

As noted at the outset, four wholly state-owned banks account for about 60 percent of bank assets, with 12 major joint-stock commercial banks, 108 city commercial banks, and more than 30,000 credit cooperatives accounting for the remainder. The main competition to the wholly state-owned banks comes from the "other commercial banks," the joint-stock and city commercial banks, in which the government also shares ownership. Even though other commercial banks

TABLE 5.3
Indicators of the Performance of State-Owned Commercial Banks
(SOCBs) and Other Nationwide Commercial Banks, 1994–2004
(percentages)

	1994–1997	1998–2001	2002–2004
Return on Assets			
SOCBs	0.1	0.1	0.3
Other nationwide banks	1.5	0.9	0.5
Return on Equity			
SOCBs	3.3	2.2	7.8
Other nationwide banks	20.7	11.0	15.4
Net Interest Income/Average Assets			
SOCBs	2.2	2.0	2.0
Other nationwide banks	3.1	2.7	2.3
Investment in securities (bonds)/Assets			
SOCBs	3.3	9.1	21.3
Other nationwide banks	10.2	14.0	20.3
Deposits with the PBOC/Deposits			
SOCBs	19.5	11.5	9.9
Other nationwide banks	24.1	26.5	14.1
Operating Expenses/Operating Income			
SOCBs	73.2	78.5	48.4
Other nationwide banks	50.3	61.4	45.9
Equity/Assets			
SOCBs	3.3	5.5	4.3
Other nationwide banks	7.7	5.5	3.1

Source: Shirai, 2001; and Fitch database.

cannot be considered truly private, they are nonetheless subject to less government direction and intervention than the
wholly state-owned banks. It is therefore useful to compare
their performance to that of the wholly state-owned banks.

Table 5.3 presents selected performance indicators for the
big four and other non-state-owned nationwide commercial
banks (principally the joint-stock banks). As the table indi-

cates, the non-state-owned commercial banks are more profitable, though their level of profitability has deteriorated since they were established in the early 1990s. The non-state-owned commercial banks are found to have better earnings on net interest income and non–interest income sources, including profits from foreign exchange transactions, and commissions from trading government bonds in the interbank market. Until recently, non-state-owned banks held a larger proportion of government bonds, revealing a greater preference for safer, more liquid assets, though pressure on the state-owned banks to improve their balance sheets has forced them to increase the share of assets they hold in government bonds in recent years. This may also indicate that other banks, lacking the extensive branch network of the wholly owned state banks, are at a relative disadvantage in retail banking markets. Also indicating that the non-state-owned banks are somewhat more cautious is that the ratio of deposits at the central bank to total deposits is higher than for the state-owned banks. Table 5.3 also shows that the non-state-owned banks are more cost efficient than their wholly state-owned counterparts, though over time the cost efficiency of the other banks has deteriorated while that of the wholly state-owned banks has increased.

Table 5.3 would seem to suggest that even a modest limitation on the extent of government intervention in bank management and practices has strong positive effects on bank performance. It is reasonable to surmise that even better outcomes would be forthcoming were a truly private banking sector permitted to develop, albeit subject to adequate supervision and regulation. Certainly barriers to entry by domestic private banks and restrictions on the scope of business and funding sources should be reconsidered and in many instances loosened or eliminated.

Privatizing and Breaking Up the State-Owned Banks

One way to instill more competition in the banking sector is to privatize the state-owned banks. Only a few years ago this was considered a radical idea, but steps are currently being taken in this direction. The China Construction Bank (CCB) was listed on the Hong Kong stock exchange in October 2005. The Bank of China (BOC) is already at an advanced stage of preparation for overseas listings. According to one observer, the BOC "could see 15% to 20% of shares floated on foreign markets, and the ICBC (Industrial and Commercial Bank of China) is not far behind" (Anderson 2005d, 34).[6]

It has also been suggested that increased competition as well as improved internal governance could be achieved by breaking up each of the big four state-owned banks into three or four smaller nationwide banks (Li 2001). It is argued that given their large size, it is impossible to impose market discipline since they are "too big to fail." As smaller entities, transparent and effective internal governance would be easier to accomplish. Importantly, as smaller entities, the banks would wield less political power and hence be less susceptible to corruption. As smaller more efficient banks, they also might be more attractive to foreign investment and to strategic partnerships with foreign banks.

Foreign Bank Entry

A major concession for WTO accession was China's agreement to fully open the domestic banking sector to foreign banks within a time span of five years. Thus in 2007, foreign owned banks will be accorded national treatment and be able to compete with domestic banks, principally the state-owned ones, on an equal playing field. What the effect will be on the banking sector overall and the implications for the currently dominant state-owned banks remains to be seen. However, there is a large recent literature on the impact of foreign bank entry in developing countries that suggests what the impact is likely to be. Before examining this literature, however, it is use-

---

[6] In November 2005, China Construction Bank issued 30.5 billion shares and raised $9.23 billion in an IPO (source: Asia Pulse).

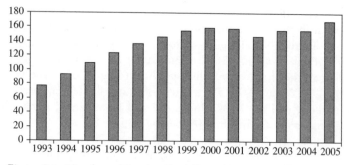

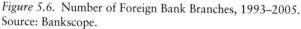

Figure 5.6. Number of Foreign Bank Branches, 1993–2005.
Source: Bankscope.

ful to review the role of foreign banks in recent years, since immediately before and since gaining membership in the WTO at the end of 2001, China has taken a number of partial measures to expand the scope of foreign bank activity in China.

The number of foreign bank branches in China, as figure 5.6 indicates, has yet to increase in spite of measures taken by the government to encourage this outcome. Moreover, most foreign bank branches have been established in the major financial centers of Shanghai, Beijing, and Shenzhen, and most are branches of banks based in the region, mainly in Taiwan, South Korea, and Hong Kong. The large international commercial banks headquartered in the United States and Europe, such as Citibank, HSBC, and Deutsche Bank, have not yet made a major move to expand their branch network in China (He and Fan 2004, 5).

Aside from setting up branches in China, foreign banks have increased their presence there by acquiring equity in a number of domestic banks, mainly the joint venture and city banks, with foreign equity in domestic banks limited to 25 percent by statute and requiring the approval of the China Banking Regulatory Commission (CBRC).[7] Foreign equity acquisition in Chinese banks has not been confined to re-

---

[7] Where the foreign equity share is equal to or exceeds 25 percent, the bank will be treated as a foreign-funded financial institution and subject to separate regulations.

gional foreign banks, but has included large multinational banks based in Europe and the United States and has been extended to both the large state-owned and other commercial banks of different size and locality.

In addition to expanding their physical presence in China, foreign banks have also been expanding the range of products they offer in the market. Foreign banks have begun to take deposits and make loans to Chinese residents, but have restricted these activities for the most part to "high-end customers" (He and Fan 2004, 8). Their main areas of activity so far, however, have been corporate banking and marketing financial derivatives. It is worth being reminded that while the level and scope of foreign bank activities in China has expanded since WTO accession, it is still relatively small and is likely to remain that way until 2007, when the foreign banks will be accorded fully national treatment.[8] What will happen then is a matter of great deal of speculation and concern in China, which is why it is useful to look at the literature to see what, in general, has occurred in other countries that have fully opened to foreign bank entry.

The literature on the impact of foreign bank entry should help to allay concerns in China. For the most part, countries that have, in recent years, undertaken aggressive financial liberalization, in which an important component was opening up the banking sector to foreign competition, have done so from a position not unlike that of China, with banking sectors dominated by state-owned banks with large portfolios of nonperforming loans. Private domestic banks in most of the countries studied in the literature suffered, as do private banks in China, from insufficient scale, inadequate technology, and poor operational and risk management practices. In spite of these weaknesses, domestic banks facing increased foreign competition have, by and large, survived it and, as the literature clearly shows, have been strengthened by it.

Three key issues are relevant—the impact of foreign bank entry on (1) competition and efficiency, (2) banking sector

[8] Foreign banks account for only about 1.5 percent of total bank assets.

stability, and (3) the allocation of credit across sectors of the economy. The literature clearly finds that foreign bank entry intensifies competition in the local banking market and as a result forces domestic banks to become more efficient. Although the profitability of domestic banks may suffer from increased foreign competition, consumers of banking services and the economy as a whole benefit from greater access to credit and better terms of borrowing (Classens, Demirguc-Kunt, and Huizinga 1998). An interesting finding in the literature, consistent with the theory of contestable markets, is that even when foreign banks' share of the domestic banking market is small, they can have a significant positive effect on competition and efficiency if their entry and activities are relatively unrestricted (Classens and Laeven 2003).

The observation that financial crises are often preceded by financial liberalization has raised concerns that, whatever the benefits of financial liberalization, it may render domestic banking systems more vulnerable and less stable (Kaminsky and Reinhart 1999). The experiences of financial crises in Latin America and East Asia suggest to the contrary that foreign bank entry is a stabilizing force. Foreign banks in developing countries, because they have more diversified portfolios and greater access to funds around the world through their parent companies, are less exposed to risk and less affected by crises in the host country. In the Latin American countries that experienced financial crises in the 1990s, foreign banks exhibited stronger growth and less volatility in their lending during crises and immediately thereafter (Goldberg, Dages, and Kinney 2000, 23). In the East Asian financial crisis, foreign banks took less risk leading up to the crisis and survived the crisis in better shape than their domestic competitors (Demirguc-Kunt, Levine, and Min 1998). Foreign bank entry, the literature suggests, promotes banking sector stability.

Foreign bank entry is also found to improve, or at least not harm, the access to credit of small and medium-sized companies (Clarke, Cull, and Peria 2001). While foreign banks tend to serve mainly larger borrowers, their impact on competition overall has the effect of improving the access to credit and the terms of borrowing of smaller companies.

It is also worth noting that the evidence in the literature suggests that foreign banks in developing countries follow their comparative advantage, concentrating their activities in certain banking niches (e.g., trade finance and derivatives) and certain branches of the economy (manufacturing), leaving domestic banks to expand in the areas of their own comparative advantage, namely retail banking, consumer credit, and lending to small and medium-sized companies. Even in countries that began with fragile and inefficient domestic banking systems, local banks have survived and even expanded in the face of increased competition from foreign banks.

Interest Rate Liberalization

While major steps have been taken to resolve the NPL problem, to improve corporate governance, and to increase competition in the banking sector, relatively little progress has been made in liberalizing interest rates. The only step in that direction was the decision of the PBOC in October 2004 to remove the ceiling on bank lending rates, though the impact of this modest step toward interest rate liberalization is as yet unknown.[9]

The principal exception to interest rate controls in China's financial sector is in the interbank bond repo (short-term repurchase agreement) market, in which interest rates have been fully liberalized and market determined since 1997.[10] We argue in the following chapter, however, that in spite of the absence of formal controls on interest rates in the interbank market, interest rates are heavily influenced by the rate set by

[9] Since the October 2004 lifting of the ceiling, PBOC data indicate that the dispersion of lending rates has increased for rural and urban credit unions, but not for the large commercial banks.

[10] In the repo market, banks exchange cash for government securities that they agree to buy and sell back at a predetermined price and date, hence the term *repurchase agreements*, or *repos*.

the central bank on excess reserves. Moreover, the dominance in the bond market by the big four state-owned commercial banks, as we argue in the next chapter, severely limits the liquidity of the market and effectively prevents the interbank market from forming a reliable benchmark yield curve.

In the market for bank deposits and loans, interest rates still play a relatively minor role. The ceiling on deposit rates and the floor on lending rates has been the government's principal mechanism for guaranteeing bank profitability and avoiding a banking crisis in a system plagued with an NPL ratio that may be as high as 50 percent. The benefits that the government derives from its strict control of interest rates are, however, achieved at a significant cost to the economy. Interest rate controls blunt the role of market forces in determining the allocation of credit and contribute to investment inefficiency and lower growth. Interest rate controls also limit banks' ability to assess and manage risk, contributing to the bad lending practices that have saddled the banking system with an excessive stock of NPLs. In addition, interest rate controls limit the central banks' ability to use market-based instruments of monetary policy, in lieu of which the central bank has depended heavily on credit rationing and other administrative controls (discussed in more depth in the final chapter). It has been suggested, for example, that "keeping interest rates fixed at artificially low levels has made a very strong contribution to boom-bust behavior in China" (Anderson 2005d, 20). Clearly there is a strong case for much more interest rate liberalization than has occurred so far. It is also clear, however, that until the government resolves the NLP problem, no significant liberalization of interest rates is likely to happen.

CHAPTER 6

Developments in the Bond Market

THE WEAKNESSES OF THE banking sector in China are well understood, and, as explained in the previous chapter, the government has made banking sector reform a high priority. The government has also acknowledged the importance in the financial system of a well-functioning bond market, but has it taken sufficient measures to remove the impediments to the market's development and to create the conditions that are necessary for it to flourish? How have the weaknesses and shortcomings of China's bond market hindered long-term growth and macroeconomic stabilization? And, finally, what policy measures are needed to allow the bond market to develop and eventually to perform its crucial role in the financial system?

6.1. THE ROLE OF A BOND MARKET

A bond market plays a number of important roles in a well-developed financial system. First and foremost, a bond market is an important mechanism for financing long-term investment. Banks also perform this function, and in a bank-dominated financial system like China's they are the principal source of formal long-term investment finance, but banks are less well suited to perform this function than the bond market because their liabilities (mainly deposits) are short term. Moreover, because their liabilities are short term, banks tend to be more risk averse and less inclined to lend for long-term investment than bondholders. Indeed the growing mismatch in the maturity of the banking sector's assets and liabilities is an important source of systemic risk in China's banking sector. The development of the bond market, with a wide range of maturities and risk attributes would, therefore, have as an important by-product the benefit of strengthening the banking sector by allowing it to focus more on the financial services in which it has a comparative advantage.

Bond markets are also an important source of government deficit finance. Because government bonds are generally the least risky assets in the system, the market price for government bonds provides an important benchmark—a reference price and yield curve—for pricing other financial assets in the system, not only nongovernment bonds, but also bank loans and other forms of debt. In order for the bond market to perform this function there must, of course, be a well-developed secondary bond market where previously issued bonds can be traded openly and transparently by a diversified investor base. The secondary market allows purchasers of long-term bonds to liquidate their assets at will and as such improves the liquidity of long-term bonds and increases their demand in the market. The benchmark yield curve that emerges from the secondary market for government bonds allows investors to invest more efficiently since it informs them of the opportunity cost of financial assets of different maturities and risk attributes.

In addition to its role in financing long-term investment and government budget deficits, as well as providing a benchmark for pricing financial assets throughout the system, the bond market is also important for the conduct of monetary policy. Government bonds in particular, but in principle any bond, can be used by the central bank to conduct open market operations to manage money supply. The weaker the bond market, the less effectively the central bank can use this instrument of monetary policy and the more it will be forced to rely on more clumsy instruments, such as changing reserve requirements of commercial banks and the interest rate they earn on required reserves.

6.2. The Bond Market in China

Although China's bond market has developed very rapidly since its initiation in the early 1980s, it nevertheless plays a

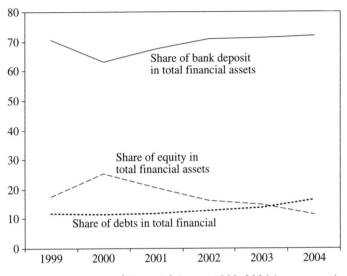

Figure 6.1. Structure of Financial Assets, 1999–2004 (percentages).
Source: CEIC.

modest role in China's overall financial system (Bottelier, 2004). As figure 6.1 indicates, the banking sector dominates the financial system, accounting for over 70 percent of total financial assets. Stocks and bonds combined account for the remainder, stock market capitalization having fallen as a share of total financial assets since 2000 as a result of the fall in stock market prices (discussed in the next chapter).

China's bond market is not only a small part of the financial system, but also is entirely dominated by the government. As of the end of 2004, as table 6.1 indicates, government bonds accounted for 97 percent of total bonds outstanding, with the remaining 3 percent mainly bond issues of state-owned enterprises and commercial banks.

Government bonds consist of treasury bonds issued by the Ministry of Finance (MOF) mainly to finance government deficits, policy bonds (referred to as *policy financial bonds* in the Chinese literature) issued by the three policy banks, principally the China Development Bank (CDB), to finance infrastructure projects, and, since 2003, short-term notes of the

TABLE 6.1
Stocks of Outstanding Bonds by Issuer, 1981–2004 (RMB 100 million)

			Percentage Share of Government Bonds				
Year	Total Stock of Bonds Outstanding	Government Bonds Outstanding	Treasury Bonds	Policy Bonds	PBOC Notes	Corporate Bonds	Other[a]
1981	49	49	100				
1985	237	237	100				
1990	1,086	890	100			195	
1995	5,560	4,914	67	33		647	
2000	21,265	20,403	64	36		862	
2001	25,161	24,152	65	35		1,009	
2002	30,460	29,390	66	34		1,070	
2003	38,946	37,630	60	31	9	1,136	180
2004	53,516	51,505	50	27	23	1,233	778

Source: CEIC and Monthly Report; China Government Securities Depository Trust and Clearing Company and http://www.Chinabond.com.cn.

[a]Includes bonds issued by commercial banks (mainly subdebt), securities firms, and other nonbank financial institutions.

People's Bank of China (PBOC) issued for the purpose of sterilizing increases in foreign reserves (discussed in detail in chapter 8).

6.3. GOVERNMENT BONDS

Bond Placement

In the 1980s, government bonds were mainly placed administratively by means of a quota system that allocated treasury bonds to the provinces in proportion to provincial revenues.[1] The provinces then allocated their quota of treasury bonds to

[1] This method of allocating quotas had the perverse effect of allocating a disproportionate share of treasury bonds to provinces for which bond acquisition had the highest opportunity cost (the richer provinces that had better alternative investment opportunities). See Gao 1999.

TABLE 6.2
Share of Treasury Bonds Held, by Category of Investor (percentages)

	1994–95	August 2005[a]
Individuals	75	0.8
Commercial bank	5	73.9
Nonbank financial institution[b]	10	18.8
Nonfinancial institution	10	0.4
Special settlement member[c]		6.1

Source: Monthly Report, CGSDTC; and http://www.Chinabond.com.cn.

[a]August 2005 data does not include 402 billion and 240 billion placed through stock exchanges and other channels for which data on the breakdown by investor are not available.

[b]Includes credit unions, investment and trust companies, securities firms, insurance companies, and funds.

[c]Includes the PBOC, MOF, and three policy banks.

subprovincial governments that in turn allocated them to the SOEs under their authority. The SOEs in turn shifted the burden of financing the treasury bond issues to their workers, providing them with bonds (or a share of the bonds the SOEs were responsible for) in lieu of wages. Thus, by 1995, 75 percent of treasury bonds outstanding were held by "individuals." While the government appealed strongly to patriotism as a motivation for holding treasury bonds, it did try to make bonds financially attractive by setting the yield at one to two percentage points above the bank deposit interest rates (Gao 1999).

In the early 1990s the government began to experiment with syndicate underwriting and competitive bidding auctions to place its bonds, but these methods did not supplant administrative placements until the mid-1990s.[2] The shift from administrative placement to syndicate underwriting and competitive bidding auctions has led to a significant diversification of investors in the government bond market. As table 6.2 indicates, especially important has been the increased participation of institutional investors.

[2] A detailed historical account of the bond market can be found in Gao 1999.

As table 6.2 indicates, commercial banks have become the principal holder of government bonds, accounting for about three-quarters of the outstanding stock. The attraction of government bonds for the commercial banks derives mainly from financial repression of the financial system. First, financial repression has insured that the bulk of financial savings in the economy flow to the banks—the banks have the money, so not surprisingly they are the main investor in government bonds. Second, with the deterioration in the financial position of the banks' traditional customers (the SOEs) in the mid-1980s and the subsequent buildup of a large stock of NPLs, the commercial banks came under strong pressure from the government to diversify and strengthen their asset portfolios. Acquiring government bonds provided the opportunity to raise asset liquidity and capital adequacy ratios. Moreover, although the yield on government bonds is significantly lower than on bank loans, the riskiness of government debt and the costs of intermediation are also significantly lower, indeed negligible. In addition, interest earned on government bonds is tax exempt. Government bonds have, therefore, become an attractive investment for the commercial banks, even though the spread between bank deposit rates and government bond yields is relatively low, as figure 6.2 indicates.

Bond Maturities

The structure of the terms to maturity (or residual terms) of government bonds is shown in figure 6.3. Short-term bonds with a maturity of one year or less are made up almost entirely of PBOC sterilization notes that have been issued only since 2003, when the PBOC found itself unable to sterilize its large and growing foreign exchange acquisitions because of an inadequate stock of short-term treasury securities in the market. The PBOC was therefore forced to sell its own debt to the state-owned commercial banks in order to absorb the excess liquidity in the banking system that resulted from its heavy intervention in the foreign exchange market.

The residual terms of treasury bonds, figure 6.3 indicates,

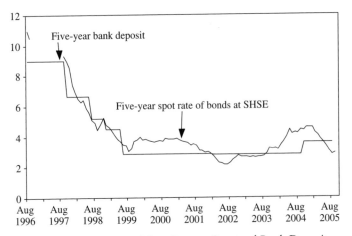

Figure 6.2. Treasury Bond Spot Interest Rate and Bank Deposit Rate (August 1996 to August 2005). Source: CEIC; Shanghai Stock Exchange and http://www.Chinabond.com.cn.

are clustered in the three- to five-year maturity range. The bulk of long-term treasury bonds with a residual maturity of 10 years or more are made up of special treasury bonds issued in 1997 to recapitalize the "big four" state-owned commercial banks (discussed in chapter 5). If we exclude these special (nontraded) long-term bonds, we see that the MOF supplies very little long-term or short-term debt to the market. An important reason why the MOF prefers multiyear to short-term maturities is that treasury bond issues are subject to an annual issuing quota, set by the National People's Congress, which the MOF can better leverage by issuing multiyear maturities than short-term ones that would require refinancing and count against the quota.[3] The MOF is also constrained in its ability to issue very long-term debt because the demand for such debt by the commercial banks, which are the majority holders of treasury bonds, is limited. The demand by the commercial banks for very long-term debt is weak because (1) the

[3] In December 2005, the quota control on issuing treasury bonds was changed to a ceiling requirement on total outstanding.

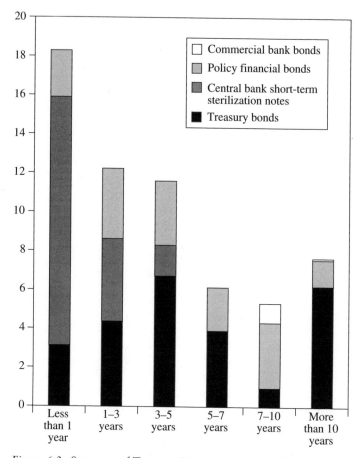

Figure 6.3. Structure of Terms to Maturity in the Interbank Market as of August 2005 (RMB 100 million). Source: Monthly Report, China Government Securities Depository Trust and Clearing Company; http://www.Chinabond.com.cn.

bank's liabilities are short term, (2) the risk premium on long-term debt is all but nonexistent (discussed below), and (3) the market liquidity for treasuries is low (discussed below).

An important part of the banking sector reform in the mid-1990s was the establishment of three policy banks, the main objective of which was to relieve the commercial banks of policy lending and allow them to operate more like conventional commercial banks. The interbank bond market has become the main channel for financing the CDB.[4] Since 1998, the issuance of policy bonds by CDB has increased very rapidly. In contrast to the PBOC and the MOF, the policy banks have issued bonds with a wide range of maturities, but favoring mid- and longer-term bonds that better suit their financing requirements for medium- and long-term infrastructure investment projects.

Bond Trading and Liquidity

In the 1980s, there was no bond market per se, as bonds were placed administratively (as explained above), although informal secondary markets where individuals and nonbank institutions voluntarily traded government debt did nonetheless emerge spontaneously. In 1988, a formal secondary market was introduced in 61 cities, and in December 1992, futures trading of the treasury bonds was introduced in Shanghai stock exchange (SHSE). As a result of a scandal, futures trading of treasury bonds was closed down in May 1995. Commercial banks subsequently became an even greater source of funds (via reverse repurchase agreements) for stock market investors and, given their dominant position in the financial system, contributed significantly to the boom in the stock market in the mid-1990s. In an effort to cool down what was viewed as an "overheated" stock market, the central government in June 1997 banned commercial banks from trading on the stock exchanges and from lending to securities firms.[5] As a result, the commercial banks withdrew to the interbank

---

[4] Unlike the CDB, the other, smaller policy banks (the China Export Import Bank and the Agriculture Development Bank) still rely heavily on direct government financing.

[5] In June 1997, PBOC promulgated the "Notice Governing the Irregular Flow of Funds from Banks into the Stock Market" and the "Notice Prohibiting Commercial Banks from Conducting Spot and Repurchase Transactions on the Stock Exchanges."

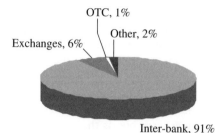

Figure 6.4. Bond Trading by Market.
Source: http://www.Chinabond.com.cn.

market, which subsequently became the dominant market for both new issues and secondary trading in government bonds, as illustrated in figure 6.4. Currently, the majority of treasury bonds, all policy bonds, and all central bank notes are issued and traded in the interbank market.

Since their recent introduction in 2003, short-term central bank notes have become the most actively traded instrument. The attraction of central bank notes, which have filled a major hole in the maturity structure of government bonds, is that because they are short-term instruments, banks and other financial institutions can use them more readily to manage short-term liquidity. It is worth noting however, that as the pressure on the PBOC to sterilize foreign reserve accumulations and refinance its outstanding debt has intensified, the maturity of central bank notes has been lengthened, as figure 6.5 indicates. As a consequence the lack of sufficient government debt at the short end of the maturity structure is still not being adequately addressed, which for reasons discussed below constitutes a major limitation in China's bond market.

As table 6.3 indicates, policy bonds, which are primarily issued by the China Development Bank, are more actively traded than the treasury bonds. Moreover, although policy bonds and treasury bonds have similar maturity structures and risk attributes, policy bonds are much more liquid than treasuries due to measures taken by the China Development Bank to improve liquidity of its bonds in the interbank

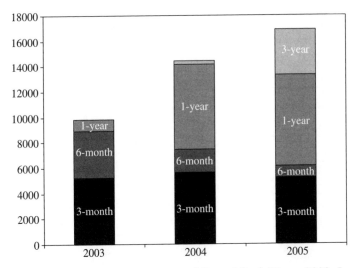

Figure 6.5. Issuing Term Structure of Central Bank Notes, 2003–5 (RMB 100 million). Source: Calculated from data provided on Bloomberg.

market, including the introduction of floating rate bonds in 1999, issuing debt debentures with option provisions in 2001, and introducing symmetrical bonds, reopening bonds, and STRIPS.[6]

Treasury bonds, as table 6.3 indicates, are the least liquid instrument in the bond market. In part this is due to the fact that the maturity structure of treasury bonds is narrowly concentrated in the mid- to long-term range. It is also the result of the trading strategy of the state-owned commercial banks that are the major holders of treasury bonds, a "buy and hold" strategy. Non-state-owned banks, in particular city and

---

[6] Symmetrical bonds are bonds with both fixed and floating rates of the same bond instrument issued at the same time with the option to swap between the two at a future time. Reopen bonds are bonds reissued with the same term structure and coupon rate as a previously placed bond. STRIPS (i.e., Separate Trading of Registered Interest and Principal of Securities) allow investors to hold and trade the interest and principal components of each bond as separate securities.

Table 6.3
Bond Market Liquidity by Instrument and Investor, 2004 and 2005

	2004				2005			
	Total Bonds Outstanding (RMB 100 m.)	Share in Total Outstanding (%)	Share in Trading Volume (%)	Liquidity Ratio[a] (%)	Total Bonds Outstanding (RMB 100 m.)	Share in Total Outstanding (%)	Share in Trading Volume (%)	Liquidity Ratio[a] (%)
By Instrument								
Total	51,625	100	100	55	72,172	100	100	88
Treasury bonds	24,177	47	19	22	27,049	37	17	40
Central bank notes	11,708	23	41	98	22,208	31	48	138
Policy bonds	13,730	27	41	79	17,698	25	26	92
Other securities	2,010	4	0.4	6	5,217	7	9	105
By Investor								
Total	51,625	100	100	55	72,172	100	100	88
Commercial banks	34,162	66	67	55	51,008	71	60	74
State-owned banks	23,607	46	25	30	46,238	64	15	21
Other banks	10,555	20	42	113	4,770	7	44	584
Other investors	17,463	34	33	53	21,164	29	40	120

Source: http://www.Chinabond.com.cn.
[a]The volume of spot market trading as a percentage of the outstanding stock of bonds by instrument and investor.

rural banks, are much more active traders, as table 6.3 indicates. Nonbank bondholders are also, on average, more active traders than the state-owned banks, with some nonbank participants very heavily engaged in active bond trading, in particular securities firms (with a liquidity ratio of 3,886 percent in 2004), SOEs (207 percent), and investment funds (158 percent).

In spite of active bond trading by non-state-owned banks and certain nonbank bondholders, the overall liquidity of China's bond market is extremely low. The low level of liquidity can be clearly traced to the most salient feature of China's financial system, the dominance of the state-owned commercial banks. State-owned banks dominate not only the banking sector, but also the bond market, where the banks' heavy involvement has limited the growth of bond market liquidity and as a result has discouraged the participation of other investors and stifled the growth of the market.[7]

Another unfortunate manifestation of the low level of liquidity in the bond market is the inability of the market to form a reliable benchmark yield curve. Normally, the pricing of treasury bonds would provide the most reliable benchmark yield curve, but because the term structure of treasury bonds is rather narrow and trading by state-owned banks that dominate the market is limited, the yield curve for treasuries is difficult to form. Neither central bank notes nor policy bonds provide a viable alternative, since both are confined to one end or the other of the maturity range. The lack of a reliable benchmark yield curve makes it difficult to measure the opportunity cost of financial assets with different term structures and credit risk attributes. As a result, bond market prices, like the prices of bank loans, cannot be relied upon to provide market signals that generate an efficient allocation of funds in the financial system.

[7] On December 15, 2005, the CDB launched the first issue of asset-backed securities (bonds) that allow non-traded assets to be transformed into traded securities, assisting banks to improve the maturity matching of assets and liabilities. CCB also launched the first mortgage-backed securities in China on the same day.

TABLE 6.4
The Annual Volume of Repo Transactions by Market, 2001–4

	Total Annual Trading Volume (RMB 100 m.)	Interbank Market		Stock Markets	
		Trading Volume (RMB 100 m.)	Share in Total Trading (%)	Trading Volume (RMB 100 m.)	Share in Total Trading (%)
2001	55,620	40,133	72	15,487	27
2002	126,304	101,885	80	24,419	19
2003	170,215	117,215	68	53,000	31
2004	137,263	93,176	67	44,086	31

Source: http://www.pbc.gov.cn.

The Interbank Money Market

The dominant and perverse influence of the state-owned commercial banks extends beyond the primary and secondary government bond market to the money market, where banks and other financial institutions use short-term repurchase agreements (repos) to manage their liquidity positions. Participants in the money market with an excess supply of liquidity can lend short term (usually with a maturity from overnight to seven days) to other participants that have an excess demand for liquidity, allowing the lenders to earn interest on money that would otherwise be idle and the borrowers to undertake business opportunities that they would otherwise have to forego. Borrowers in the money market typically use treasury bonds as collateral to secure their loans, with an agreement to repurchase the collateralized bonds (and hence repay the loan) at maturity.[8]

The growth of repo transactions in the interbank and stock markets is shown in table 6.4. The volume of repo trading increased rapidly in 2002, when the central bank expanded

[8] A relatively small volume of money market transactions between very large institutions is conducted in the bank offer market, which serves the same function as the repo market, but where loans are not collateralized.

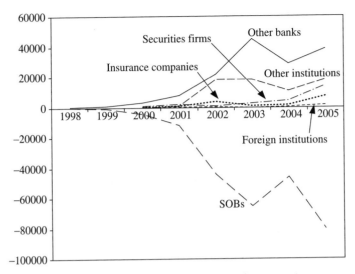

Figure 6.6. Volume of Net Repo Transactions, by Institution, 1998–2005 (RMB 100 million). Source: http://www.pbc.gov.cn; Li and Yin 2005; http://www.Chinabond.com.cn.

credit with the aim of accelerating growth and declined significantly in 2004 when monetary policy was reversed to slow down the "overheated" economy (discussed in detail in chapter 8).

Because of their privileged status in the financial system, the state-owned commercial banks alone among all the participants in the money market have been in the position of having an excess supply of liquidity, which, as figure 6.6 indicates, they have transferred via repo transactions to non-state-owned banks and other financial institutions in the system that typically have an excess demand for liquidity.

The volume of repo trading between the state-owned commercial banks, on one side of the market, and other banks and financial institutions, on the other, naturally depends on overall credit conditions. However, a particularly important determinant of conditions in the repo market is the interest rate that banks, in particular state-owned commercial banks

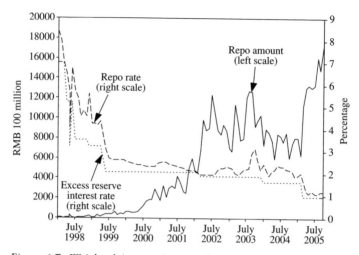

Figure 6.7. Weighted Average Repo and Excess Reserves Interest Rates, January 1998–July 2005. Source: http://www.Chinabond .com.cn.

that typically have excess liquidity, earn on excess reserves they hold at the central bank. The excess reserves interest rate, set by the central bank, constitutes the opportunity cost to the state-owned commercial banks of lending excess liquidity in the repo market. Not surprisingly, as figure 6.7 indicates, the interest rate in the interbank repo market follows closely the interest rate the central bank sets on excess reserves. When the interest rate on excess reserves is lowered, the repo rate declines and the volume of repo transactions increases. Since that volume is high relative to spot trading in the bond market, the interest rate of excess reserves has a major influence on short-term bonds and on yields throughout the market. Consequently, the government bond market, which is generally perceived to be the most liberalized part of the financial system, remains very much under the indirect control of the government and will remain so as long as the state-owned commercial banks dominate the market and excess reserves are paid interest.

6.4. CORPORATE BOND MARKET

The one function of the bond market that China needs most urgently—financing long-term corporate investment—China's bond market performs hardly at all. As noted above, the stock of outstanding corporate bonds accounts for only about 2 percent of total bonds outstanding. Moreover the current outstanding stock of corporate bonds is almost entirely the issues of centrally controlled state-owned enterprises. Before 1993, corporate bond issuance was largely unregulated and was undertaken mainly by locally owned SOEs that sold the bulk of the bonds they issued (with guarantees by their corresponding commercial bank) to employees. Since 1993, the responsibility for strictly controlling the quantity and terms of corporate bond issues has rested with the State Planning Commission and its successor, the National Development Reform Commission (NDRC), which views corporate bonds as a tool to serve industrial and regional investment projects that get funding from the NDRC. The NDRC sets a quota for corporate bond issuance, and sets the interest rate at a level no higher than 140 percent of the deposit interest rate for the same maturity.

Currently the bulk of corporate bonds outstanding is held by insurance companies and investment funds, commercial banks having been banned from investing in corporate bonds with the promulgation of the Commercial Bank Law (1995, amended 2003). Secondary trading in corporate bonds is done in the interbank market and on the stock exchanges, but the liquidity of the secondary market is exceptionally low, as most corporate bonds are held by the original investors to maturity. The maturity of the bulk of corporate bonds is in the range of 10 to 20 years, but the yield varies little with maturity. In other words, there is no curve in the corporate bond yield curve. It is obvious that, given the restrictions that currently apply, the corporate bond market cannot become an important source of financing long-term corporate investment.

However, removing controls on issuance, purchasing, and corporate bond yields is only part of the solution.[9] In order for corporate bonds to become a viable source of finance for long-term investment, the government must develop the market infrastructure, including a liquid secondary market, a transparent information disclosure system, a reliable credit rating system, compliance with accounting standards, and the requisite legal remedies, such as an effective bankruptcy law, foreclosure procedures, and an effective court enforcement system. In addition to all of these measures, the bond market needs to escape the clutches of the four big gorillas that dominate the entire financial system, the big four state-owned banks. Development of the bond market, therefore, depends on successful reform of the banking sector. It is also the case that banking sector reform would be facilitated by development of the bond market, which would allow banks to reduce the fundamental systemic risks that arise from the mismatch between their assets and their liabilities.

6.5. CONCLUSION

As noted at the outset, bond markets have several important functions in a well-developed financial system, financing long-term investment, financing government deficits, providing instruments for the conduct of monetary policy, and providing a reference price and benchmark yield curve for pricing debt. Currently, the bond market mainly serves but one of these functions, financing government deficits and priority infrastructure investment projects. It does not serve at all as a mechanism for financing long-term corporate investment; it has failed to generate a reliable benchmark yield curve; and it is unable to supply adequately the financial instruments the central bank needs to conduct open market operations effec-

[9] The PBOC introduced corporate short-term financing notes in the interbank market and the total issuance amount has exceeded RMB 100 billion, close to the amount of the total outstanding of corporate bonds issued since 1997 (which was 122.3 billion at the end of 2004).

tively. These shortcomings of the bond market were of less consequence when the economy was centrally planned and ownership was largely limited to state-owned enterprises, but they constitute a significant obstacle to long-term growth and a potential threat to macroeconomic stability (discussed in detail in chapter 8) in the current circumstances in China.

CHAPTER 7

The Rise and Fall of the Stock Market

A WIDESPREAD PERCEPTION of the general public worldwide is that bonds are boring, stocks are sexy. Not surprisingly, China's stock market, unlike its bond market, has attracted much attention since it was established in Shanghai in 1990 and Shenzhen in 1991.[1] In its short 15-year history, China's stock market has experienced a full boom-bust cycle. The first 10 years saw market capitalization grow from next to nothing to RMB 4.8 trillion in the year 2000, an amount equivalent to 25 percent of total financial assets and 54 percent of GDP. Since then, from 2000 to 2005, the market capitalization has fallen to RMB 3.7 trillion, which in 2004 amounted to only 12 percent of total financial assets and 26 percent of GDP.

Since its establishment, the stock market has been the subject of an ongoing debate among policymakers, market analysts, and investors, with the focus in the 1990s on the causes and consequences of its "overheating," and since 2000 on the causes and consequences of the market's sharp and prolonged decline. In this chapter we revisit that debate, which can be conveniently separated into two analytical phases: the bull market of the 1990s and the bear market since 2000. Given the focus of this study, we examine how the stock market has performed, in both its bull and bear phases, as a source of investment financing, as a means for enforcing corporate governance, and as a mechanism for signaling information about publicly listed companies to investors. At the heart of the

---

[1] As the economic reform urged the enterprises to find financial sources other than budget to finance their investments, some enterprises started to issue stocks to their employees and the public as early as 1984. Voluntary trading was rampant until the central government established SHSE and SZSE in the early 1990s.

matter, of course, is the question of whether the market's rise and fall reflected changes in market fundamentals, shifts in government policy, or possibly the "irrational exuberance" of investors.

In chapter 4 we noted that about two-thirds of outstanding shares of publicly listed companies are nontradable. These are shares held by the state (in the State Assets Supervision and Administration Commission, SASAC) and by so-called legal persons, which consist of state-owned enterprises, shareholding companies, and nonbank financial institutions. Tradable shares consist of A-shares that are held by Chinese nationals and traded in the domestic market, B-shares that are purchasable in foreign exchange and are mainly held by foreigners, and H-shares and N-shares that are foreign currency-denominated and traded on the Hong Kong and New York exchanges, respectively.[2] In the domestic stock market the bulk of trading is in A-shares, the focus of our examination.

7.1. The Rise

Growing Number of Listed Companies

In the 1990s the stock market became a source of funding for a growing number of companies. As figure 7.1 shows, in the five-year period from July 1995 to July 2001 the number of securities listed on the two exchanges rose almost fourfold, from about 300 to over 1,100. Most of the companies listed during this period were state-owned or formerly state-owned, privatized companies in which the state was a dominant shareholder. According to one study (Zhang 2004), 80 percent of listed companies are under state control. The listing of shares is subject to the approval of the China Securities and Regulatory Commission (CSRC), which gives priority to state-owned enterprises, especially the larger ones. Since these are

[2] B-shares were opened to domestic investors with foreign exchange in February 2001. Source: http://English.people.com.cn.

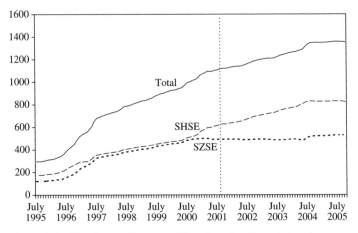

Figure 7.1. Number of Securities Listed on the Shanghai and Shenzhen Exchanges (SHSE and SZSE), 1995–2005. Source: CEIC and Datastream.

the companies that have preferred access to bank credit and bond issuance, the rapid expansion of the stock market in 1990s did little to ease financial repression in the economy.

Growing Number of Individual and Institutional Investors

The enthusiastic response of the investing public to the emergence of the stock market in the 1990s, even one dominated by state-owned or controlled firms, is a clear indication of just how repressed was the demand on the part of financial investors for nonbank assets.[3] As figure 7.2 indicates, at the peak of the market in July 2001, the number of individuals' stock accounts had risen to about 63 million, while the number of accounts held by institution investors stood at about 300,000.

[3] Such excess demand can be reflected in the price differentiations of A- and B-shares: they are identical, but the investors are different (A for domestic investors and B for foreign investors). For example, foreign investors paid only about one-quarter (for B- or H-shares) the price that domestic investors paid for the counterpart A-shares (Fernald and Rogers 1998).

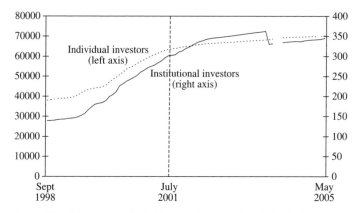

Figure 7.2. Number of Individual and Institutional Stock Accounts, September 1998–May 2005 (thousands). Source: CEIC and Datastream.

Soaring Prices the First Ten Years Running

The enthusiasm with which investors embraced China's newly emerging stock market is reflected in the dramatic rise in the average share prices on the two exchanges, shown in figure 7.3. Between July 1995 and July 2001, when the market collapsed, average share prices increased almost fourfold, a 30 percent annual rate of increase. It is not hard to understand the investors' enthusiasm for stocks. Before the stock market was introduced in the early 1990s, there was no way that individual savers could reap more than a small fraction of the returns that were being earned by those investing China's savings. The stock market offered an opportunity for ordinary people to get a piece of the new wealth being generated in China's rapidly expanding economy. It would not be surprising if, with no previous experience in a stock market, Chinese investors' perception was that a stock market moves in one direction only—up. After all, for the first ten years of its existence that is the only direction it moved. Not only in China, but elsewhere in the world stock markets boomed in the 1990s. High and rising price-earnings ratios (PE ratios) on the two exchanges, as figure 7.4 indicates, did little to discourage investors until the market collapsed in mid-2001.

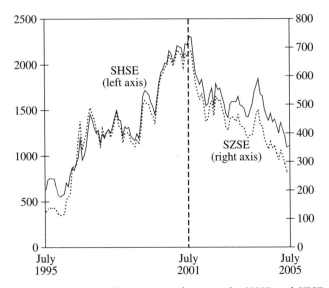

Figure 7.3. Average Share Price Indexes on the SHSE and SZSE, July 1995–July 2005. Source: CEIC and Datastream.

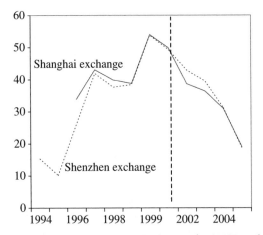

Figure 7.4. Price-Earnings Ratios on the SHSE and SZSE, 1994–2005. Source: CEIC and Datastream.

The Role of Commercial Banks

The dramatic rise in stock market prices was not only the product of investor exuberance. Commercial banks also played a major part in driving the market up. In the mid-1990s, as the stock of bad loans began to mount, the commercial banks began to look for new profit opportunities and found them in the stock market. Such was the volume of commercial bank stock trading and lending to securities firms that the government, fearing that the market was overheated, took steps to limit the commercial banks' access to the stock market in 1995, announcing that bank funding of stock traders through the repo market would be closely supervised. The banks found a way around this limitation, however, by setting up investment companies and investing in the market through their regional branches. In 1997, the PBOC began to monitor and supervise commercial banks more rigorously and forced the commercial banks to withdraw completely from spot and repo trading on the stock exchanges. The measures taken in 1997 are believed to have contributed to the leveling off of share prices from 1997 to 1999 (see figure 7.3), but the impact on the market was only temporary. Prices resumed their upward trend thereafter as the banks found new ways around the restrictions, for example by lending working capital to SOEs that used the bank funds to finance stock purchases.[4] The influential journal *Securities Market Weekly* reported that anywhere from RMB 300 to 600 billion of commercial bank funds flowed to the stock market in the year 2000 alone.[5]

Short-Term Trading and Role of the "Stock Bankers"

The surge in stock prices in the 1990s clearly reflects the dominance in the market of short-term speculative trading. The short-term returns on A-shares in the 1990s were the

[4] A study by the Ningbo branch of the PBOC identified ten channels through which commercial bank funds flowed to the securities markets in violation of regulatory prohibitions (http://www.people.com.cn, June 4, 2001).

[5] http://finance sina.com.cn, November 27, 2001.

highest in the world. Initial returns (the percentage difference between the issue price and the first-trade price) were as high as 1,000 percent in the early days of the market, and averaged over 200 percent throughout the 1990s (Gu 2003). Moreover, the stock turnover rate in China's A-share market was exceptionally high in the 1990s, with the average hold time of A-shares of one to two months, as compared to 18 months in the U.S. stock market (Xu and Wang 1999).

Not only did individual investors treat the market as a casino, but institutional investors did so as well. Among the institutional speculators were, however, a significant number who rigged the game by acquiring large positions in particular stocks that allowed them to manipulate prices and earn enormous returns at the expense of individual investors, the so-called stock bankers (*zhuang jia*). Although the media reported extensively on the activities of stock bankers and a number of books were published that illustrated how individual investors could profit by following the trading of the stock bankers, there is very little formal analysis of their impact on the market.[6] One exception is a study by Shu and Bin (2002), who found that the degree of concentration of ownership of a particular stock was the single most significant variable explaining changes in stock market prices. Their econometric results showed that the higher the concentration of ownership and the smaller the company, the higher the stock price. Indeed, after controlling for concentration of ownership, stock prices (in the 1990s) showed only a weak relation to company performance, for which Shu and Bin used as a proxy the change in earnings per share.

7.2. THE FALL

The rise in market capitalization in the 1990s, as figures 7.5 and 7.6 indicate, was almost entirely due to a rise in share

---

[6] The best illustration of the stock banker phenomenon is a 22-installment TV series called *Stock Banking* [*Zuo Zhuang*] that was widely broadcast.

Figure 7.5. Share Price Index and Market Capitalization on the SHSE, July 1995–July 2005. Source: CEIC and Datastream.

Figure 7.6. Share Price Index and Market Capitalization on the SZSE, January 1993–January 2005. Source: CEIC and Datastream.

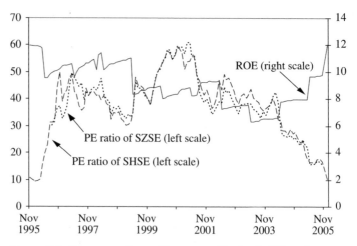

Figure 7.7. Percentage Rate of Return on Equity (ROE) and Price-Earnings (PE) Ratios on the SHSE and SZSE, November 1995–November 2005. Source: CEIC and Datastream.

prices rather than growth in the number of shares issued. With the market "correction" after July 2001, the level of market capitalization collapsed together with stock market prices. As shown in figures 7.1 and 7.2, after July 2001, growth in the number of listed shares slowed dramatically and growth in the number investors came to a halt.

Fundamentals

As noted above, the financial fundamentals of listed companies appear to have had little to do with the stock market boom in the 1990s. It is therefore not surprising that fundamentals also appear to have little to do with the collapse of the market in 2001. As figure 7.7 indicates, price-earnings (PE) ratios show no relation to average corporate rate of return on equity (ROE). Indeed, as figure 7.8 indicates, the stock market boomed during an economic slowdown and collapsed during the recent economic boom, which commenced in 2002 and peaked in 2004. In spite of the rise in corporate

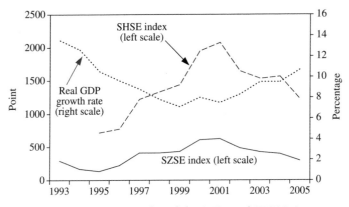

Figure 7.8. Real GDP Growth and the SHSE and SZSE Price Indexes, 1993–2005. Source: CEIC and Datastream.

profits during the 2002–4 upswing (discussed in detail in the next chapter), China's stock market remained moribund with little or no sign of an impending rally. We must therefore look elsewhere for an explanation of the loss of investor confidence that led to the fall and prolonged stagnation of China's stock market.

Contagion

One possible source of the loss of investor confidence in China may have been the collapse of stock market prices in the United States and other countries in the region in 2001. See figures 7.9 and 7.10. The year 2001 was not, however, the first highly publicized stock market downturn in neighboring countries to occur after the establishment of China's stock exchanges. The Asian financial crisis of 1997–98 led to sudden, dramatic declines in the stock market prices across the region, but not in China, where stock prices merely leveled off in 1998 and 1999, perhaps as much due to the pullout from the market of commercial banks as from contagion effects of the Asian financial crisis. Even Hong Kong and India, which were not seriously affected by the Asian financial

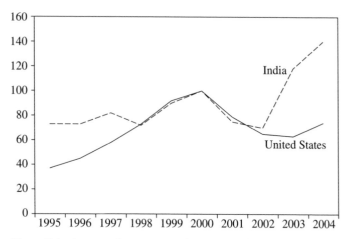

Figure 7.9. Average Share Price Indexes in the United States and India, 1995–2004 (2000 = 100). Source: IMF, *International Financial Statistics*, selected volumes.

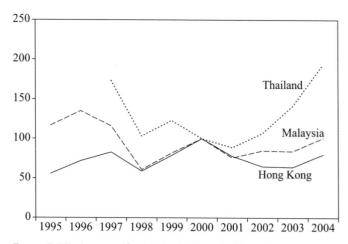

Figure 7.10. Average Share Price Indexes in Hong Kong, Thailand, and Malaysia, 1995–2004 (2000 = 100). Source: IMF, *International Financial Statistics*, selected volumes.

crisis, saw their stock markets temporarily decline in its wake. The 2001 downturn was, however, deeper and more prolonged than that in 1998. However, as figures 7.9 and 7.10 indicate, the U.S. and Asian markets began to recover in 2002 and 2003, while China's stock market continued to decline and remains depressed (as of mid-2005) in spite of the fact that PE ratios had fallen from a high of 60 at the peak of the market in 2000 to a very reasonable 15 by mid-2005. We are led to the conclusion, therefore, that while contagion no doubt played a role, there were clearly other factors that led to the collapse of investor confidence in China's stock markets.

Scandals and Market Improprieties

As noted above, illegal stock price manipulation by so-called stock bankers played a significant role during the stock market boom of the 1990s. It is also commonly alleged that listed firms falsified accounts and cooked the books to artificially inflate their stock prices (Shirai 2002). Not surprisingly, these practices inevitably led to several highly publicized scandals that erupted in 2001 and severely undermined investors' confidence in the market. The first major scandal involved two "stock bankers" who borrowed RMB 540 million from banks, enterprises, and individuals to manipulate the price of Zhong Ke Chuang Ye (SZSE code 0048), which rose from 15 yuan on October 27, 2000, to 84 yuan two months later, after which, in just 20 days, it fell to 11 yuan. On January 11, 2001, the CSRC undertook an investigation and a week later referred the case to the Beijing public security bureau.[7]

A second major case involved the company Yin Guang Xia, which was revealed in August 2001 to have been falsifying its accounts in order to drive up the price of its stock, which in the year 2000 rose 440 percent. The CSRC's investigation and referral of the case to the public security authorities was also highly publicized.[8] One of the "stock bankers"

[7] Source: http://news.xinhuanet.com, June 11, 2002.

[8] Source: http://finance.sina.com.cn/nz/ygx/index.html: this website has a summary of the news related to the Yin Guang Xia case.

in the Yin Guang Xia case was a financial investment company affiliated with the Ministry of Finance (China Economic Development Trust and Investment Company), which in 2003 was closed down by the PBOC for a string of regulatory violations in the stock market.[9] Indeed, even the China Securities Regulatory Commission itself was hit with scandal when, in 2004, it was revealed that an official in charge of reviewing and approving IPOs was taking bribes.[10] Since the market collapsed in June 2001 there has been a stream of revelations of fraudulent accounting, illegal price manipulation, regulatory violations, and corruption in China's stock market, all serving to undermine investors' confidence.

Selling State Shares

It is clear that the government's strategy in establishing and encouraging the growth of the stock market in the 1990s was to provide a mechanism for privatizing state-owned enterprises while at the same time maintaining state control over the privatized companies by reserving for itself the majority of issued shares, which were held outside of the market. In 2001, the government's strategy changed fundamentally with a decree by the State Council on June 12, announcing the government's intention to begin selling previously nontradable state-owned shares in listed companies. The motivation for this shift in strategy was primarily the growing fiscal strains in China's social security system. As we explain in the following chapter, China faces a large and rapidly growing pension liability, the financing of which will require the government to liquidate its enterprise assets if it is to avoid a fiscal crisis in the future. The State Council decree was an initial, modest step in that direction.

It is reported that a number of plans for liquidating state ownership were considered in early 2001, including one that would have made a large one-time transfer of two trillion

[9] Source: http://news.xinhuanet.com, June 8, 2002; and http://economy .enorth.com.cn, November 13, 2003.

[10] *Caijing* magazine, issue 121, November 29, 2004.

yuans' worth of shares (equivalent to 21 percent of GDP) to the state pension fund (Naughton 2002). A more modest plan, and the one that was ultimately adopted in mid-June 2001, called for the selling off of RMB 10 to 20 billion in state shares annually, which although not a solution to the long-term problem would nonetheless have plugged the immediate hole in the pension fund. When the State Council issued the implementing regulation for the plan on June 14, 2001, the Shanghai index was at an all-time high of 2,200—what better time to sell the People's assets!

The market did not, of course, wait for the state to begin selling off its shares, but instead reacted immediately with a 25 percent decline over the following three months. The drop in the market following the announcement of the government plan to sell off state shares led the leadership to waver on the plan (Naughton 2002). To insure that the plan would be abandoned, representatives of more than 20 securities firms reportedly "gathered secretly . . . and decided to dump shares in a concerted effort to force the market down" (Naughton 2002, 6). The market plunged further, and the strategy worked. On October 22, 2001, just four months after its announcement, the CSRC announced the suspension of the plan to float state shares.

The suspension of the plan to sell off state shares did not, however, restore investors' confidence, as most came to the view that the state was simply biding its time until share prices increased to resume the floatation of state shares. A random market poll of investors by Hua Ding Market Investigation Company in 2002 found that the main concern of most investors was a resumption of the plan to sell off state-owned shares in the market.[11]

The state did not resume the plan to sell off state shares until fall 2005, although it did take a series of measures designed to boost stock prices. For example, in June 2003, the government gave permission for the National Council for Social Security Fund to invest in the stock market; in April

[11] Source: http://www.xinhuanet.com.cn, January 22, 2002.

2004, permission to enter the stock market was granted to insurance companies, and in June 2004 it was expanded to allow securities investment funds to invest in the stock market; in January 2005, the stamp duty on financial transactions was cut by half to encourage stock trading. In addition, a small window was opened to foreign funds through the Qualified Foreign Institutional Investors (QFII) in May 2003, albeit subject to the quota control by the State Administration of Foreign Exchange (SAFE). None of these measures has had the intended effect, as the market continued to fall, hitting its all-time low in June 2005, with the Shanghai indexed at 1,091, half of what it was four years earlier. It is apparent that investors have interpreted government measures to boost stock prices as a prelude to the full floatation of state-owned shares.

After many vain efforts to boost stock prices since the market downturn in mid-2001, the Chinese government resumed the selling off of state nontradable shares in fall 2005, accompanied by further steps to expand market access by potential investors, the most recent such measure allowing foreign "strategic" investors and investment funds to invest directly in the stock market if they agree not to sell the shares they purchase for three years. So far (as of late 2005), none of these measures, neither the limited floatation of state shares nor the broadening of investors' access to the market, has had any impact on market fundamentals, as the market remains at or close to its all-time low.

7.3. Conclusion

The current state of China's stock market reflects the misguided strategy the government took in initiating it, which was to create an alternative mechanism for raising funds for state-owned and state-controlled enterprises. As a result the stock market has failed to provide a channel for financing long-term corporate investment. With the majority of shares in state hands, the stock market has also failed to serve as a means for enforcing corporate governance and improving enterprise efficiency. Weak regulation and supervision allowed stock bankers to manipulate prices, listed companies to engage in fraudulent accounting practices, and officials to abuse the public trust. If this were not enough to destroy investors' confidence, the prospect of a massive flooding of the market with state-owned shares has driven investors from the market. Until the government changes its strategy fundamentally, it is unlikely that China's stock market will play a significant role in the financial system.

CHAPTER 8

Macroeconomic Policy and Performance

THE MAIN FOCUS OF THIS study has been long-term growth in China—what initiated it, what has driven it, and what is needed to sustain it. We have argued that what initiated the acceleration of long-term growth was a process of step-by-step institutional reforms that led to the marketization of the economy, improved incentives, and more efficient resource allocation. We have argued that what has driven growth, as well as structural change, technological change, and employment growth, is investment. What fueled investment was mainly rising saving rates in the household and business sectors. We have argued that what is required to sustain growth is liberalization and development of the financial sector, which, as we explained in the preceding chapters, is a matter to which the government has given a high priority, committed considerable resources, and made progress in recent years, although it still has much to in both the banking sector and financial markets.

In this final chapter we shift the focus from the long run to the short run. Our aim is to explain the ups and downs of the economy rather than long-term growth. We give particular attention to the role that government policy, macroeconomic policy in particular, has played in fueling and dampening major swings in the macro economy. We argue that investment has not only been the engine of long-term growth, but also the main source of "boom-bust" cycles in China. Furthermore, we argue that the underdevelopment of the financial sector is not only an obstacle to sustainable long-term growth, it is also a source of short-term instability and an impediment to effective macroeconomic stabilization policy. Ongoing reforms in the financial sector are beginning to moderate the macroeconomic cycle and make macroeconomic policy more effective,

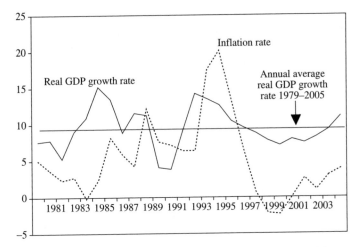

Figure 8.1. Real GDP Growth and Inflation Rates, 1979–2004 (percentages). Source: *China Statistical Yearbook* 2004 and for the year 2004, Anderson 2005a.

but further reforms are needed to give policymakers the tools they need to keep the economy on a high and stable growth path.

8.1. UPS AND DOWNS IN THE MACRO ECONOMY

China's economy is sometimes described as one of repeated "boom-bust" cycles, but as figure 8.1 indicates, that description is not particularly apt. Real GDP growth has exceeded 7 percent every year since the reform process began in 1979, save two, 1989 and 1990, when it was at 4.1 and 3.8 percent, respectively. Booms China has had, but busts, at least in terms of what the word is usually meant to describe, it has avoided. A more apt description of China's macroeconomic cycles might be surges and retrenchments, of which three major ones are apparent since the early 1980s: 1985–91, 1992–96, and 2002–the present (mid-2005), the latter not yet fully played out.

China also has an enviable record of price stability, with only four years—in the 25-year period since reforms began—of double digit inflation: 1988 (12.1 percent), the peak of the first cycle, and 1993–95 (averaging 17 percent), at the peak of the 1992–96 cycle. Since 1995, the inflation rate has averaged just below 2 percent. Indeed, from 1997 to 2000, the inflation rate was at or below zero, which raised concerns about deflation and deficient aggregate demand, albeit that real GDP was growing at the same time at 8.6 percent on average. While the inflation rate rose to 24 percent at the apex of the previous cycle, 1992–96, in the most recent one it peeked at only 3.6 percent in 2004 and appears to be headed down to about 2 percent in 2005 as the economy attempts a "soft landing" from the 10.5 percent growth rate it reached in 2004.

8.2. Investment Spending as the Proximate Cause of Macroeconomic Cycles

Macroeconomic cycles are not caused by—but instead are represented by—the acceleration and subsequent deceleration of aggregate investment and consumption spending by the public and private sectors. In China, as figure 8.2 indicates, macro cycles are principally the product of cycles in investment spending, consumption growth rising and falling with the growth of real income. Investment spending is, however, what has sparked the upturns and downturns in the macro economy.

Investment is only the proximate cause of China's macro cycles, the underlying causes being those factors that have led to accelerations and decelerations in investment spending. Before we offer an explanation of what underlies the cycles in investment spending, it is useful to examine the cycles more closely.

It is a widely held view that macroeconomic cycles in China are mainly generated by government-directed investment in state-owned enterprises: when the government wants

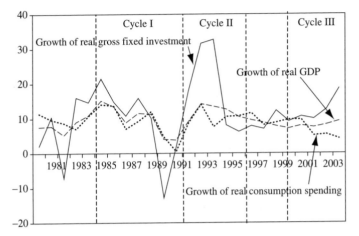

Figure 8.2. Growth of Real Fixed Investment and Consumption Spending, 1979–2003 (percentages). Source: *China Statistical Yearbook* 2004.

to stimulate the economy, it transfers funds or directs bank credit to SOE investment, and when it wants to cool down the economy, it reverses these administrative measures. If this view were valid, one would expect to observe that SOEs contribute disproportionately to investment expansion and contraction in the upswings and downswings of the cycle, or more precisely that in the upswing (downswing) the rate of growth of SOE investment (g_I^{SOE}) is higher (lower) than the rate of growth of total investment (g_I^{TOT}):

$$\text{in the upswing: } \frac{\Delta I^{SOE} \,/\, \Delta I^{TOT}}{I^{SOE} \,/\, I^{TOT}} = \frac{g_I^{SOE}}{g_I^{TOT}} > 1$$

$$\text{in the downswing: } \frac{\Delta I^{SOE} \,/\, \Delta I^{TOT}}{I^{SOE} \,/\, I^{TOT}} = \frac{g_I^{SOE}}{g_I^{TOT}} < 1$$

Interestingly, the conventional wisdom about the source of macro cycles in China appears not to be valid. As figure 8.3 indicates, non-SOEs appear to contribute more to acceleration and deceleration of investment than do the SOEs. Indeed, a

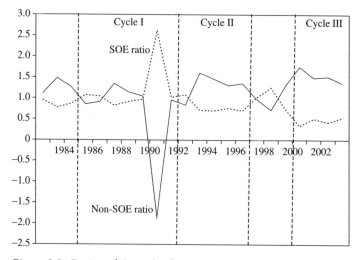

Figure 8.3. Ratios of Growth of Investment by SOEs and Non-SOEs to the Growth of Total Investment, 1982–2002. Source: *China Statistical Yearbook* 2004.

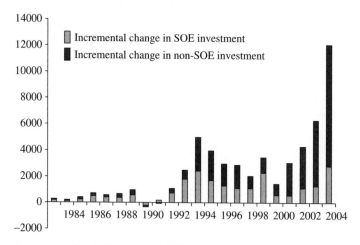

Figure 8.4. Annual Incremental Change in Investment by SOEs and Non-SOEs, 1982–2003 (RMB 100 million). Source: *China Statistical Yearbook* 2004.

cursory look at figure 8.3 suggests that investment spending by SOEs has become increasingly countercyclical, rising and falling less in the upswing and downswing than non-SOE investment. Indeed, in the acceleration phase of the current cycle, from 2000 to mid-2004, the average annual growth of SOE real investment was 7 percent, or less than one-third the rate of growth of non-SOE real investment (24 percent). As figure 8.4 indicates, the main impetus to the 2002–3 investment boom was non-SOE (mainly private) investment, even though the popular perception based on press reports was that the investment boom was the product of government-directed credit to a few key sectors (steel and autos in particular).

8.3. Anatomy of Macro Cycles in China

The Underlying Cause: The "Hunger for Investment and Drive for Expansion"

In a Western market economy, the common assumption is that firms maximize profits and households maximize utility. On the basis of this assumption, central banks use a money-based interest rate policy to manage aggregate demand by firms and households, raising interest rates during the upswing of the business cycle to dampen investment and consumption spending and lowering them in the downturn for the reverse effect.

In China's state-dominated, financially repressed economy, on the other hand, interest rates are fixed at below the market clearing level, excess demand for credit is the norm, and funds are rationed. Moreover, the main objective of China's state-owned and state-dominated firms, so it has been argued, is not to maximize profit but instead to maximize "investment growth and the drive for expansion" (Zou 1991). This is only rational since the reward to bureaucrats who manage state-owned and state-dominated enterprises is not the profit they earn, but mainly the prestige, power, and accompanying perks they derive from commanding an organization, which are the greater the larger the organization.

Even in an autocratic state there is, however, a political price to pay if sufficient heed is not given to the welfare of the people and the stability of the economy, which constrains the bureaucrats' drive for expansion when an investment boom leads, as it inevitably does, to accelerating inflation and imbalances in the real economy. At this point the authorities begin to put the breaks on and the economy descends with a hard or soft landing, as the case may be. The interaction of these two competing objectives (expansion and stability), as Zou (1991) has demonstrated in a formal model and tested on Chinese data, is the investment cycle that was prominent during the central planning era and has endured since then, albeit with diminishing intensity.

The 1992–97 Cycle: How It Played Out

In 1991, after two years of relatively low growth and growing political unrest, motivated in part by the relatively poor performance of the economy in the preceding two years, authorities in China began to accommodate the rising demand for investment spending by both the central and especially local governments. In 1992, bank lending for investment increased almost 50 percent (see figure 8.5). Already, by 1993, inflationary pressure began to mount and the authorities began to tighten credit and limit investment approvals, but by then enterprise profits were rising and firms dramatically accelerated investment through retained earnings and other internal sources, which together with a devaluation of the currency in 1994 served to spur growth and boost inflation to over 20 percent in 1994.

Two years later, in 1996, the inflation rate was down to 7 percent and investment growth was one-third of what it was in 1993. A continuing squeeze on credit and limits on investment approvals slowed and eventually, in 1995, halted the growth in investment credit. At the same time, as figures 8.6 and 8.7 indicate, excess capacity began to build up in key sectors, inventories began to mount, and enterprise profitability began to shrink, limiting firms' ability to finance investment

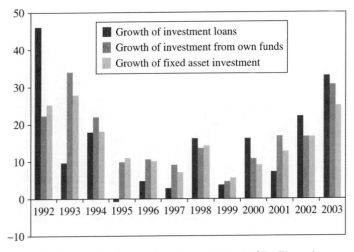

Figure 8.5. Growth of Fixed Asset Investment and Its Financing from Bank Loans and Own Funds, 1992–2003 (percentages). Source: *China Statistical Yearbook* 2004.

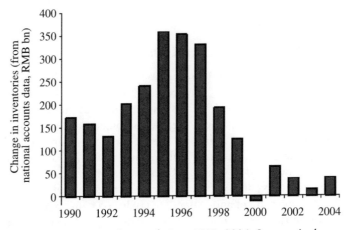

Figure 8.6. Inventory Accumulation, 1990–2004. Source: Anderson 2005e, 2.

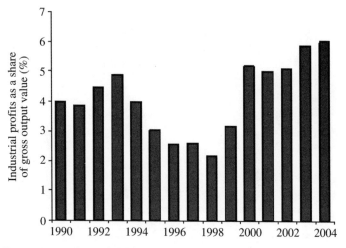

Figure 8.7. Industrial Profit Margins, 1990–2004. Source: Anderson 2005e, 2.

out of retained earnings. Declining investment demand, excess capacity, and a good harvest in 1996 served to halt inflation altogether in 1997.

The 2002–Present Cycle: Similarities and Differences

From the end of the previous cycle in (1996) to the beginning of the current cycle (2000–present) China weathered the Asian financial crisis (1997–98) and a global economic slowdown (2000–2001). These events, combined with continued weak profits in the industrial sector, led to investment and GDP growth that, although high by most countries' standards, were below trend in China. In 1998, the authorities began to engineer an expansion by approving increased levels of government investment and expanding credit. As figure 8.5 shows, the response was an immediate acceleration of growth in real fixed investment and bank loans to finance it. The 2000–2004 upswing also saw a pickup in company profits and a substantial increase in investment financing out of retained earnings and other internal funds. Already by mid-2003, however, concerns began to mount about the "overheating" of the economy, as the real GDP growth and inflation rates increased. Immediately, the authorities began to take administrative and market-oriented measures to "cool down" the economy. Amazingly, in just a matter of two or three years, China's most widely recognized macroeconomic problem was reversed from one of "deflation" to one of "overheating" and inflation.

One can see similarities between the two cycles, but the differences are greater. One of the most striking is the disproportionate contribution of the nonstate sector to the investment boom in the current cycle as compared to previous cycles, as shown in figures 8.3 and 8.4. Another major difference is the rate of acceleration of inflation accompanying the two cycles. Even though rate of growth of investment and GDP (in constant prices) in the current cycle has been almost as high as in the previous one and, what is more, from a higher overall level of investment as a percentage of GDP, the accompanying acceleration of inflation was insignificant compared to that in 1993–94. Third, unlike the previous investment boom, the current one did not lead to any significant increase in inventories after the cycle peaked, though it is reported that excess capacity and inventory accumulation did occur in several heavy industries where government-directed investment was particularly strong (steel, autos, cement, and aluminum). Fourth, while both cycles are associated with increased profit rates in the upswing, there is no evidence of a significant decline in profits after the current cycle peaked, as there was in the previous cycle.

Explaining the Anatomical Differences in the Two Cycles

It is reasonable to suppose that macroeconomic policymakers in China are likely to achieve a more benign outcome and a softer, smoother landing in the current cycle because they have learned from the past and have acted more promptly. There is no reason to dispute this supposition. We would argue, however, that what explains the superior performance in

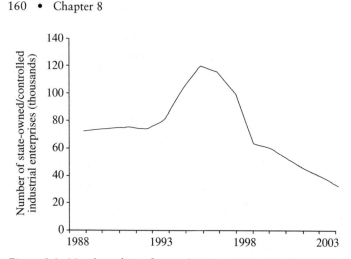

Figure 8.8. Number of Nonfinancial SOEs, 1988–2003. Source: Anderson 2005b, 12.

the current cycle is not just better macro management (which we examine below), but, perhaps even more important, the far-reaching structural reforms that were made in the wake of the previous cycle. Among these reforms and structural changes, the more important include the following:

- *SOE reforms.* Since 1995, the government has taken a number of measures to make SOEs more accountable for their profits and losses, as well as to subject them to a threat of bankruptcy and closure. The number of SOEs has declined by about half since the mid-1990s through closures, management buyouts and downsizing. As a result, the SOE share of industrial output and employment has declined dramatically since the mid-1990s. (See figures 8.8 and 8.9.) It is reasonable to assume that the SOEs that survived the massive downsizing after 1995 are, on average, more efficient and profitable, which may in turn explain why in the current cycle there was no widespread buildup excess capacity or inventory accumulation, and why profit rates have held up through the cycle.
- *Banking sector reforms.* Since the mid-1990s measures have been taken to reduce government interference in bank lending decisions (especially at the local level). Banks are no longer

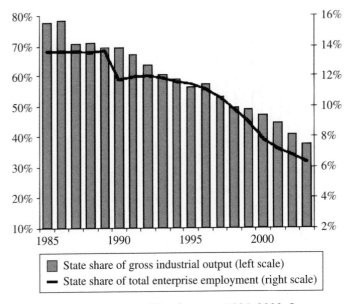

Figure 8.9. SOE Output and Employment, 1985–2003. Source: Anderson 2005b, 12.

obliged to finance SOE losses, as they were during the downturn of the 1992–96 cycle, when the bulk of the banks' nonperforming loans were accumulated. As result of the improved performance of SOEs and the improved lending practices of the banks, the stock and flow of NPLs are diminishing. Thus we observe in figures 8.10 and 8.11 another important difference in the current cycle, the avoidance of a buildup of bad debt in the banking system.

- *Increasing competition.* Most SOE monopolies in China have been at the local and provincial level, protected by interprovincial tariff and nontariff barriers. Since 1994, however, as part of its effort to recentralize the fiscal system, the central government has forced the provinces to dismantle such barriers, with the effect of significantly increasing domestic competition. Not only has domestic competition increased, but with China's entry into the WTO, international competition has intensified as well. Indeed, since the early 1990s, the average tariff rate has fallen from about 45 percent to 10 percent (see figure 1.5).

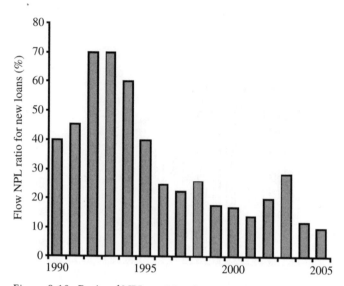

Figure 8.10. Ratio of NPLs to New Loans, 1990–2005.
Source: Anderson 2005d.

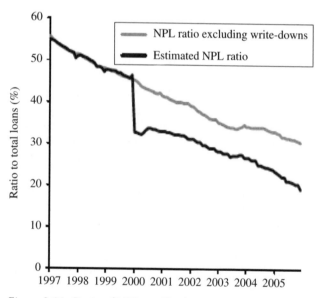

Figure 8.11. Ratio of NPLs to Total Loans, 1997–2005.
Source: Anderson 2005d.

- *Increasing openness.* Trade liberalization has not only intensified competition, it has led to a significant increase in the importance of foreign spending for domestic production in China. As figure 8.12 shows, the ratio of exports to GDP rose from about 20 percent in 1997 to over 30 percent in 2004. Some unknown proportion of exports represents the reexport of imported intermediate inputs used in export production and hence does not represent foreign spending on domestic value-added. If we assume that 25 percent of the gross value of exports represents reexports of imported intermediate inputs, then the ratio of domestic value-added exports to GDP shows a rise from about 15 percent in 1997 to 27 percent in 2004. Put another way, domestic expenditure on domestically produced goods (netting out expenditure on imports) accounted for about 70 percent of total expenditure in 2004, as compared to 85 percent just six years earlier. As figure 8.13 indicates, in the downswing of the present cycle, from mid-2004 onward, foreign demand played a crucial role in sustaining growth in spite of the decline in domestic spending following measures taken by the government to cool the economy down.

  The increasing openness of China's economy, especially since it gained membership in the WTO in 2001, has clearly had an important stabilizing effect in the recent macro cycle. Growing openness has promoted market diversification and consequently has dampened the impact of cycles in domestic spending on growth. Of course, with growing openness, China's economy becomes more vulnerable to the vagaries of the world market. However, since China is, for the most part, a price-taker in the world markets for most of the goods it exports, fluctuation in global business conditions can be expected to have a relatively modest effect on China's economy.

- *Growing importance of the private sector.* Between 1998 and 2003 the share of the private firms in the business sector value-added increased from 53 to 63 percent. Over the same five years, the share of private firms in nonfarm business sector value-added increased from 43 to 57 percent (OECD 2005, 81). Indeed, as indicated in figure 8.3, non-state-owned firms accounted for about 80 percent of the increase in investment in

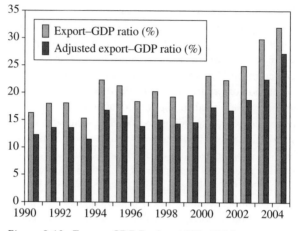

Figure 8.12. Export-GDP Ratios, 1990–2005.
Source: *China Statistical Yearbook* 2004, 2005.

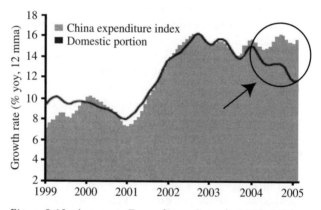

Figure 8.13. Aggregate Expenditure Growth, 1990–2005.
Source: Anderson 2005a, 2.

2003. Given China's heavy reliance in the past on administrative measures rather than market-based instruments of macroeconomic management, the increasing importance of the private sector has no doubt weakened the government's ability to conduct macroeconomic policy by traditional means. The effectiveness of administrative measures of macroeconomic control has also been weakened by measures taken by the government itself, such as the shift in July 2004 from a positive to a negative investment regulation regime, allowing firms to invest in any project that is not explicitly prohibited rather than, as in the past, only in projects that are explicitly allowed (World Bank 2004, 12). In light of these altogether salutary developments, the decontrol of interest rates becomes all the more essential for providing the government with the tools it needs to manage aggregate demand and maintain a stable macro economy.

8.4. MONETARY POLICY

Money, Credit, and Inflation

It was observed above that investment-growth cycles have been accompanied by a rise and fall in the inflation rate. We have also noted that the authorities in China have used credit supply to spark and rein in investment growth. It is therefore not surprising that this blunt instrument of monetary policy has produced sharp swings in the rate of inflation. In China, as elsewhere, inflation is a monetary phenomenon, as figure 8.14 indicates. Variation in the growth of M2 (mainly currency in circulation, and demand and saving deposits in the banking system) and bank claims (mainly the stock of outstanding loans) on the nongovernment sector of the economy closely parallel variation in the inflation rate.

As figure 8.14 indicates, there is, on average, about a 15 to 20 percentage point spread between the rate of money growth and the inflation rate. According to the quantity theory of money, the inflation rate is roughly equal to the difference between the rate of growth of supply and demand for money. The difference between the money growth rate and the inflation rate is therefore a rough measure of the rate of growth of demand for money balances, which as we explained in chapter 4 has been extraordinarily high in China due to the rapid

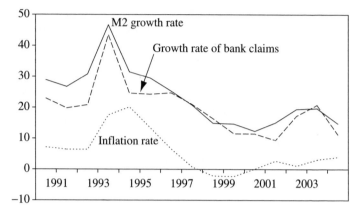

Figure 8.14. Rates of Growth of M2, Bank Claims, and the Inflation Rate, 1990–2004 (percentages). Source: *China Statistical Yearbook* 2004.

growth of the economy, high and rising saving rates, urbanization, and the measures the government has taken to repress financial markets and insure that the bulk of financial savings flows to the banking system.

Money Creation and Seigniorage

Supplying money is a closely guarded monopoly of (almost) every government and for good reason—supplying money is one means by which the government finances its spending and thereby gets claim to the national product (GDP). The claim on the national product that the government derives from creating money is known as *seigniorage*. In China, seigniorage amounts to about 6–8 percent of GDP, which is about four to five time greater than in most other market economies.[1] Seigniorage is exceptionally high in China for the same reasons that the growth of demand for money is excep-

---

[1] The measure used here is the change in base money as a percentage of GDP.

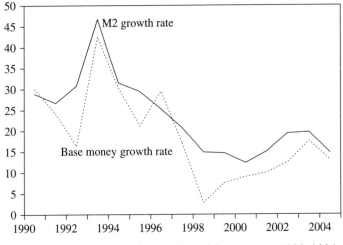

Figure 8.15. Rates of Growth of M2 and Base Money, 1990–2004 (percentages). Source: *China Statistical Yearbook* 2004.

tionally high—growth in the economy, structural change, and financial repression. Indeed, as we suggested in chapter 4, governments repress their financial systems for the principal purpose of maximizing their claim on the national product through seigniorage and other means.

The central bank creates money by accumulating domestic and foreign financial assets, in the process of which deposits are created in the banking system and the money supply expands. The assets of the central bank constitute the base of the money supply, the money supply being a multiple of the base. A figure 8.14 indicates, the money supply (M2) and base money grow together at roughly the same rate.

The accumulated stock of the foreign assets by the central bank is the nation's official foreign reserves. The domestic financial assets that central banks accumulate are usually government debt, but in China are mainly claims on (or loans to) commercial banks, mainly the state-owned ones. In China the central bank does not directly finance the government's budget deficit by "printing money" (buying government debt),

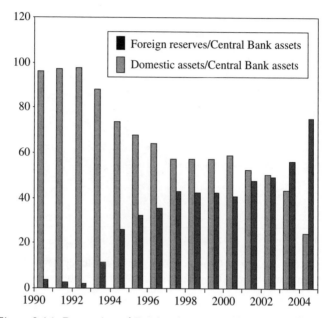

Figure 8.16. Domestic and Foreign Assets as a Percentage of Total Central Bank Assets, 1990–2005. Source: *China Statistical Yearbook* 2004.

but it does so indirectly since the state-owned commercial banks to which the central bank lends are the principal purchasers of government debt, as explained in chapter 6. As figure 8.16 indicates, since the mid-1990s the central bank has substantially reduced the rate of growth of domestic claims while at the same time substantially increasing its holdings of foreign reserves, which between 1990 and 2004 increased as a share of central bank assets from 3 percent to 75 percent. As explained in chapter 6, since 2003 the central bank has been obliged to issue its own debt to the commercial bank to sterilize reserve accumulations and avoid excessive growth in reserve (base) money, as illustrated in figure 8.17.

The dramatic increase in foreign reserves is mainly a by-product of China's policy of pegging the value of the RMB to the U.S. dollar. In order to keep the dollar exchange rate

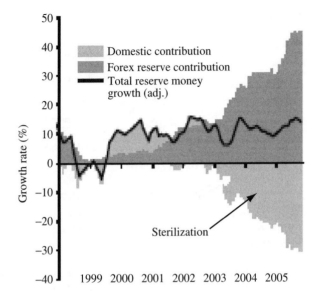

Figure 8.17. Growth of Reserve Money and Its Components, 1998–2005 (percentages). Source: Anderson 2005a.

fixed, the PBOC is obliged to buy up excess supplies of foreign exchange that result from trade and current account surpluses and net inflows of foreign capital, which since the mid-1990s have been enormous and have led to the accumulation of about $750 billion in foreign reserves by mid-2005. The accumulation of foreign reserves leads inextricably to an expansion in the domestic money supply and potentially to an acceleration of inflation. To avoid that outcome the PBOC has had to offset the increase in foreign reserve assets by reducing the rate of accumulation, in some years (e.g., in 2004) the absolute amount, of domestic assets, a policy maneuver known as "sterilized intervention"—sterilizing the impact of foreign reserve accumulation so as to avoid the inflationary consequences of the money supply expansion that would otherwise result. The rapid shift in the structure of the PBOC assets has put severe strains on China's anti-inflationary monetary policy and led to calls for more exchange rate flexibility

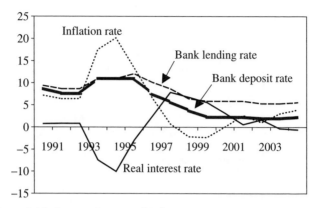

Figure 8.18. Interest Rates and Inflation, 1990–2004 (percentages). Source: IMF, *International Financial Statistics*, Yearbook 2004 and November 2005.

in order to gain more control over the money supply. China's current account surpluses and massive sterilized reserve accumulations have also attracted criticism from the United States, Europe, and Japan, which charge that China is practicing "exchange rate protectionism"—a policy of purposefully undervaluing domestic currency to gain a commercial advantage in world markets, an issue we address below.

Inflation and Interest Rates

As we have noted repeatedly, the one sector of the economy where prices are still strictly controlled is the financial sector. The only interest rates not controlled are the interbank market rates, which are fully market-determined. In the banking sector, both deposit and lending rates are subject to floors and ceilings, though on October 29, 2004, the government abolished the ceiling on lending rates.

Although interest rates are fixed, they are nonetheless adjustable and indeed have been changed repeatedly, as figure 8.18 indicates. In a market economy, the interest rate bears a close relation to the inflation rate according to the Fisher Effect, which states that the nominal interest rate is equal to the real rate of return plus the expected rate of inflation. In China, the monetary authorities have indeed changed the interest rate in response to changes in the inflation rate, but as figure 8.18 indicates, they have done so only with a lag, giving rise to significant swings in the real interest rate.

The fluctuations in the real interest rate that have resulted from the practice of fixing the interest rate and adjusting it with a lag to the inflation rate give rise to highly distorted signals in the credit market. It is also apparent from figure 8.17 that the movement of the real interest rate has been strongly pro-cyclical, falling during upswings in the economy and rising during downswings, although these perverse movements in interest rates have exerted relatively little influence on the macroeconomic cycle since rationing has been the principal mechanism of credit allocation. In recent years, however, monetary authorities have begun to limit their intervention in credit allocation and have encouraged banks to adopt market-oriented lending policies. It is doubtful, however, whether these policy changes will have the desired positive effect of improving credit allocation and contributing to macroeconomic stabilization until interest rates are more fully decontrolled. Liberalizing interest rates is, however, not something that is likely to happen until the insolvency of the banking system is rectified, since the controls on interests are what insure the liquidity of banks and prevent a banking crisis in China (as explained in chapter 5).

8.5. Capital Flows and Exchange Rate Policy

The "Impossible Trinity"

There is a proposition in international monetary economics known as the "impossible trinity," which maintains that it is impossible in the long run for a country to simultaneously (1) maintain a fixed exchange rate, (2) conduct an independent monetary policy, and (3) allow unrestricted international capital mobility. Inevitably a monetary policy aimed at domestic objectives will lead to a divergence between domestic and foreign interest rates or shifts in exchange rate expectations that will induce capital flows that the central bank will have to monetize, thereby abandoning its monetary policy. If the country is unwilling to abandon its monetary policy, then it must either abandon its exchange rate peg or restrict capital flows.

The only escape from the "impossible trinity" is sterilized intervention, which works only temporarily, especially for counties sterilizing reserve losses, since reserves will eventually be depleted, forcing the country to abandon the fixed exchange rate regime. Countries like China that sterilize reserve accumulations can, in principle, sterilize almost indefinitely, but at an ever rising cost since the interest rate the central bank pays on the debt it issues to mop up liquidity will rise relative to the interest rate it earns on its foreign reserves. It is even possible that a surplus country could be forced to abandon sterilized intervention if the balance sheet of the central bank deteriorated to the point that it could no longer sell its debt. It is therefore impossible to avoid the force of the impossible trinity indefinitely. The validity of this proposition has been proved time and again throughout history, as one country after another has been forced to abandon fixed exchange rates in order to preserve monetary policy as a tool of macroeconomic management.

In principle, China has accommodated the impossible trinity by restricting, but not completely prohibiting, international capital mobility. Attracting foreign direct investment is, of course, an important policy objective in China, and it has been greatly successful, as figure 8.19 indicates, but inflows and outflows of non-FDI are largely prohibited. However, as figure 8.19 also indicates, significant net flows of non-FDI capital have, in spite of prohibitions and strict controls, occurred in both directions. For a decade, from 1993 to 2002, China experienced net outflows of non-FDI capital, which from 1997 to 2001 were significant enough to more than offset the net FDI inflows and give China a capital account deficit, an anomaly we discussed in chapter 3 and attributed

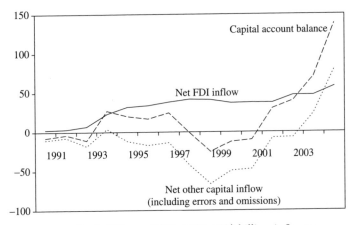

Figure 8.19. Capital Flows, 1990–2004 (US$ billions). Source: IMF, *International Financial Statistics*, Yearbook 2004 and September 2005.

in large part to financial repression. Since 2002, however, net non-FDI capital flows have reversed direction and flowed inward in significant amounts, presumably in expectation of an RMB appreciation. The inability to restrict capital inflows has as a result put China on the horns of a dilemma—abandon the exchange rate peg or abandon its anti-inflationary monetary policy, the premise being that China cannot, or at least should not, sterilize reserve accumulation indefinitely.

In the case of China, the pressure on the exchange rate and by extension the pressure to accumulate reserves derives not only from capital inflows but also from current account surpluses, which as figure 8.20 indicates have prevailed every year but one (1993) since 1990 and have been rising rapidly since 2001. Indeed, as figure 8.20 shows, surpluses on both current and capital accounts have increased significantly since 2000. The counterpart of these surpluses is of course increases in official reserve assets, which reached $820 billion at the end of 2005 and, as noted above, constitute about 75 percent of the central bank's assets.

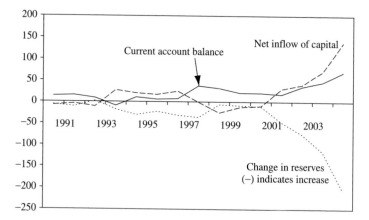

Figure 8.20. The Balance of Payments, 1990–2004 (US$ billions). Source: IMF, *International Financial Statistics,* Yearbook 2004 and September 2005.

Whither the RMB?

No issue has been debated more heatedly in recent years than the question: whither the RMB? Before we take up this question, it is useful to look at the facts. Figure 8.21 presents the nominal RMB-dollar exchange rate and the nominal and real effect exchange rates indexes from 1990 to 2004.[2] Officially, China defines its current exchange rate arrangement as a "managed float," but since 1996 the PBOC has intervened in the foreign exchange sufficiently to keep the rate fixed within a very narrow band around 8.3 RMB/$; hence the current regime is more commonly referred to as a "de facto dollar peg."

From 1988 to 1994 China had a dual exchange rate system in which the official fixed rate coexisted with a market-determined rate in so-called swap centers where exporters

---

[2] Nominal and real "effective exchange rate" indexes and trade-weighted averages of indexes of bilateral nominal and real (adjusted for relative inflation) exchange rate indexes.

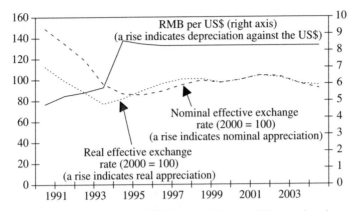

Figure 8.21. Nominal RMB/$ Exchange Rate and Nominal and Real Effective Exchange Rate Indexes, 1990–2004. Source: IMF, *International Financial Statistics*, Yearbook 2004 and September 2005.

and importers could transact with each other at the market-determined exchange rate. The RMB/$ exchange rate shown in figure 8.21 for the period prior to 1994 is a weighted average of the official and swap exchange rates, with the weight shifting in favor of the swap rate as the volume of transactions in the swap centers grew in relative importance. In 1994, China unified and devaluated the exchange rate at 8.7 RMB/$, but allowed the currency to appreciate to 8.3 RMB/$ between 1994 and 1996. The rate remained at this level until July 2005, when the authorities revalued the currency by 2 percent and announced that it would henceforth manage the exchange rate against a basket of currencies rather than against the dollar alone.[3]

Pegging the currency to the dollar means that the RMB floats together with the dollar against all other currencies in the world. As figure 8.21 indicates, from 1990 to 1993 the

[3] In the three months since that announcement, the RMB has remained fairly constant at about 8 RMB/$.

RMB depreciated in value in both nominal and real terms. In 1994, the RMB was devalued by about 48 percent, but in real terms appreciated due to high inflation in China. The currency continued to appreciate on average against most major currencies, as did the dollar to which it was pegged, until 2001, when it began to depreciate significantly along with the dollar. The real depreciation of the RMB and accompanying increases in trade and current account surpluses since 2001 are what have led to demands by the United States, Europe, and Japan that China float its currency, or at least allow more exchange rate flexibility, or at the very least revalue the exchange rate, which it did on a modest scale in July 2005.

Some of the arguments made by foreign governments in support of these demands are, simply put, nonsense. The assertion that a policy of pegging to the dollar constitutes illegal exchange rate manipulation and gives China an unfair advantage in world markets is absurd. Countries are free to choose whatever exchange rate arrangement they prefer. Indeed, pegging to the dollar was the central feature of the Bretton Woods system that governed international monetary arrangements for the first 25 years after World War II and is a practice that has been adopted by any number of countries in recent years. The United States has also claimed that by pegging the RMB to the dollar, China has contributed to high and rising current account deficits in the United States, also a bogus claim since U.S. current account deficits are mainly the result of a growing gap between expenditure and income in the United States, for which a revaluation of the RMB would be of little or no consequence. Indeed, the peg to the U.S. dollar has meant that the dollar is the only major currency against which the RMB has *not* devalued since 2001.

There are, however, good reasons for a more flexible exchange rate policy, and the more convincing ones are those that appeal to China's own national interest. If over time it becomes increasingly difficult and costly to sterilize increases in foreign reserves, appreciation of the real exchange rate may be inevitable in any case as a result of higher inflation, which is a less preferable way of achieving a real appreciation than via a change in the nominal exchange rate. Exchange rate flexibility would not only give China more control over its monetary policy, it would also allow the exchange rate to play a greater role in macroeconomic stabilization. An appreciation of the currency during the recent "overheating" episode would have worked to reduce aggregate demand and lessened the need for the government to rely on relatively clumsy administrative measures to rein in aggregate expenditure.

China has not yet experienced difficulty in sterilizing foreign reserves, and given interest rate controls and government ownership of a large part of the banking sector, it may be able to carry out sterilized intervention for quite some time. Sterilized intervention is, however, likely to become increasingly difficult to maintain as the country implements financial liberalization measures, including decontrolling interest rates and privatizing state-owned banks. Even if there is no immediate threat to China's ability to conduct sterilized intervention, the present may nonetheless be an auspicious time to begin to implement a more flexible exchange rate policy, since abandoning a pegged exchange rate is much easier to do in good times, when the country has an overall balance-of-payments surplus and is accumulating reserves, than in bad times, when it has overall balance-of-payments deficit and is losing reserves. When times are good, it is easy to believe they will last forever, but recall that Thailand and Malaysia had very strong balance-of-payments positions just a few years before the Asian financial crisis erupted in 1997.

There are good reasons not only for exchange rate flexibility, but also for maintaining a fixed exchange rate, though most of those arguments are losing strength in China. One of the main reasons for adopting a fixed exchange rate in most countries is to avoid excessive inflation by anchoring the domestic price level to a foreign (e.g., U.S.) one. This argument does not apply well in China's case, however, since it is the exchange rate peg that currently is the main source of inflationary pressure.

The strongest argument for pegging the RMB to the dollar—at a rate that by most estimates implies RMB undervaluation of about 30 percent—is that this practice is important to China's highly successful export-oriented industrialization drive that has absorbed millions of previously unemployed rural workers in productive employment.[4] If China adopts a more flexible exchange rate policy, the concern is that currency appreciation could undermine that strategy. That concern is mitigated, however, by several considerations. First, real appreciation of the exchange rate may be inevitable no matter which exchange rate regime China chooses, as we argued above. Second, while China still has a pool of rural unemployed of about 150 million, labor shortages and rising real wages are already emerging, especially in those areas where labor-intensive, export-oriented industry is concentrated (the coastal provinces). Finally, it should be recognized that if a significant real appreciation should occur, it would tilt incentives in favor of production for the domestic market, which is growing rapidly and has the potential to grow even faster, providing employment opportunities for those who would otherwise be drawn to export-oriented industry.

The currency peg has served another socially valuable function. By allowing China to accumulate upwards of $800 billion in foreign reserves, it has provided protection against a future currency crisis. China's reserves also constitute an important stock of liquid wealth that the government can draw on to finance exceptional outlays, such as to recapitalize the banking system or to meet other future contingent liabilities (discussed below). The main qualification to this benefit is that there is an opportunity cost to reserve accumulation, which is given by the difference between the return the nation earns on its foreign reserves relative to the return that would be earned if they were invested at home. It is hard to say what the optimal level of reserves is, but given the relatively low return that China earns on its foreign reserves, it is likely that at almost $800 billion, or almost twice the amount of imports in

---

[4] Frankel (2005) estimates that "the yuan was undervalued by approximately 35% in 2000, and is by at least as much today."

2004, the level of current reserves is at, or perhaps even beyond, the optimal level already.

We are led therefore to the conclusion that a policy of gradually increasing exchange rate flexibility is in China's national interest. Eventually, once the financial system has been liberalized and developed, China will likely choose a freely floating exchange rate regime, which is generally considered the preferable option for a large economy that constitutes an optimal currency area. In the meantime, China will likely find the best option to be something in between the two extremes of fixed and floating exchange rates, in other words an adjustable peg or a managed float, but with rather more flexibility than has been allowed in the recent past.[5]

8.6. FISCAL POLICY

Fiscal Decentralization and Recentralization

No aspect of China's economic transformation has received more attention than fiscal reform. As we suggested in chapter 1, the sweeping decentralization of the fiscal system undertaken in the early 1980s induced a surge of investment and growth, in particular by providing incentives for the establishment of the township and village enterprises (TVEs) that became the driving force of industrial growth until the early 1990s (Cao, Qian, and Weingast 1999).

Fiscal decentralization also had deleterious effects, however. As noted above, it induced competition among local governments, which led to the proliferation of provincial monopolies protected by interprovincial trade barriers (Young 2000b). In addition, it led to a decline in consolidated tax revenue collection over the 1980s, resulting from the inherently low tax buoyancy of the fiscal contract system, exacerbated by undercollection of taxes due to the granting of excessive tax breaks

[5] This is in fact the policy the government announced in July 2005, though it remains to be seen how it will be implemented.

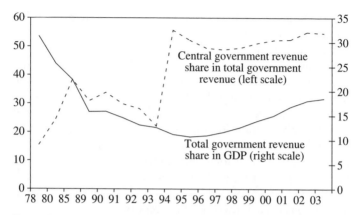

Figure 8.22. Government Revenue as a Percentage of GDP and Central Government Revenue as a Percentage of Total Government Revenue, 1978–2003. Source: *China Statistical Yearbook* 2004.

and tax holidays to the SOEs by local tax administrators (Jin and Zou 2003). As figure 8.22 indicates, government revenue to GDP fell from almost 30 percent in 1980 to as low as 12 percent in 1995. The decline in local and central government tax revenues put enormous pressure on the PBOC to print money to finance the provinces' "drive for expansion," leading to the rapid acceleration of inflation in the early 1990s.

In an effort to regain control over credit creation, increase government revenues, and raise the central government's share of them, a major fiscal reform package was introduced in 1994. The de facto "tax farming" system introduced in the early 1980s, under which the central government gave tax-raising authority to the provinces in exchange for a negotiated share of the revenues they collected, was replaced by a new system based on tax assignments and tax sharing.[6] A new value-added tax (VAT) was introduced, with the central government taking about 75 percent of the revenues col-

---

[6] *Tax farming* is the term used to describe the taxation system employed in ancient Roman and Ottoman empires, whereby private contractors were given responsibility for tax collection (farming) in return for a lump-sum payment to the public treasury. See Jin 2003.

lected. Business taxes, income taxes, and trade taxes also became subject to new sharing arrangements that favored the central government. In addition, tax administration was reformed in 1994, giving the State Administration of Taxation the responsibility for collecting central and shared taxes. As figure 8.22 reveals, the 1994 reforms led to a dramatic increase in both overall revenue collection (as a percentage of GDP) and the share of the central government in total revenue.

The 1994 fiscal reform, while centralizing government revenue collection, left the burden for the bulk of government expenditures (about 70 percent of total) at the provincial and local levels. Indeed, over the past decade the expenditure burden of local governments has increased, as many social expenditures (e.g., education and health) previously borne by SOEs have been transferred to local government as part of the industrial restructuring process (Fedelino and Singh 2004, 31). To fill the gap between provincial revenue and expenditure, the central government provides fiscal transfers and subsidies to local governments, which amount to about 45 percent of local government resources. A recent IMF study concludes, however, "Despite their large size, transfers have nonetheless proved inadequate to provide sufficient financial support to the provision of essential services such as rural education and rural public health" (Fedelino and Singh 2004, 39).

Government Deficits and Debt

The growth of government revenue as a percentage of GDP since the mid-1990s has been accompanied by an even higher rate of growth of government expenditure and, as figure 8.23 indicates, the emergence since the mid-1990s of budget deficits averaging about 3 percent of GDP. Government budget deficits have largely been financed by issuing domestic government debt, which as figure 8.24 shows, has risen to a level of about 30 percent of GDP.

The persistence of budget deficits raises the issue of whether China's fiscal position is sustainable. In other words, under current circumstances, will the government debt ratio

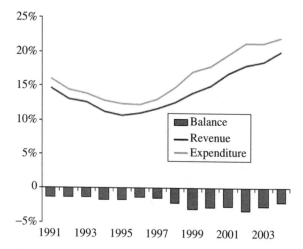

Figure 8.23. Revenue, Expenditure, and the Budget Balance, 1991–2004 (percentage). Source: Anderson 2005c, 32–33.

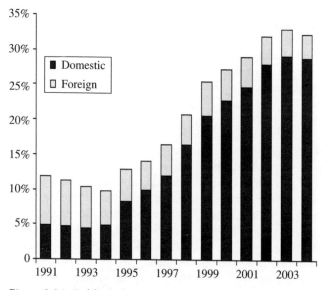

Figure 8.24. Public Debt as Percentage of GDP, 1991–2004. Source: Anderson 2005c, 32–33.

continue to rise, possibly to a level that if unchecked could undermine macroeconomic stability?

Two things can be said with confidence about this issue. First, China's government debt ratio by international standards is relatively low. In other Asian emerging market economies, it is about three times higher, on average (Fedelino and Singh 2004, 29). Second, under current circumstances, it is not likely to increase significantly. The government debt-GDP ratio is stable when it is proportional to the ratio of the fiscal deficit as a percentage of GDP and the GDP growth rate (a ratio of about 3 to 10 or 30 percent), which is approximately the current debt-GDP ratio.[7] We can conclude, therefore, that as long as the government deficit as a percentage of GDP does not rise or the growth rate does not fall, China's fiscal position is strong and constitutes no immediate threat to macroeconomic stability.

Future Threats to Fiscal Stability

The problem with "other things being equal" pronouncements is that often other things turn out *not* to be equal, and in the case of China a number of potential threats to its fiscal position loom in the future. One we discussed in chapter 5 is the implicit liability of the government to recapitalize the banking sector, the cost of which by most estimates is about 15 to 20 percent of GDP. This, however, is not the only future liability the government faces. In addition, there are the contingent liabilities of SOEs and local governments that the central government could be required to assume, amounting to a sum as larger or larger than the cost of bailing out the banks.

The greatest threat to future fiscal stability is, however, the government's unfunded pension obligations. The fiscal challenge China faces in meeting its implicit future pension obliga-

---

[7] $$\Delta \frac{D}{Y} = \frac{D}{Y}\left(\frac{\Delta D}{D} - g\right) = \left(\frac{G-T}{Y}\right) - \frac{D}{Y} \cdot g. \quad \Delta \frac{D}{Y} = 0 \text{ if } \frac{D}{Y} = \frac{(G-T)/Y}{g},$$

where D is the stock of government debt, Y is GDP, g is the GDP growth rate, and $(G - T)$ is the government budget deficit.

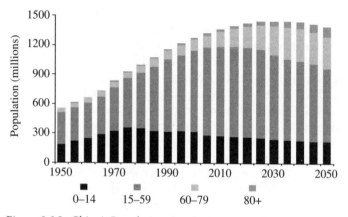

Figure 8.25. China's Population Age Structure, 1950–2050 (projected). Source: Anderson 2005c, 32–33.

tions is similar to that of other countries that, like China, have a declining population growth rate and a rapidly rising dependent population ratio, combined with a relatively well-developed social security system (relative to other developing countries, that is). The difference is that other countries confronting this challenge, like Germany and Japan, have per capita income levels many times that of China. In comparison to other developing countries, however, the fiscal challenge from China's implicit future pension obligations is especially onerous for two reasons. First, as a result of its unique one-child policy, China has become an ageing country well before its time, as the share of the working-age group in the population has already peaked and is beginning to fall, while the absolute number and percentage share of the aged is rising rapidly (see figure 8.25). Second, because of its socialist roots, urban workers, especially those employed by state-owned enterprises, have enjoyed cradle-to-grave security, often referred to as the "iron rice bowl," which is an implicit, if not explicit, liability of the government. Furthermore, in recent years the government has widened the social security net to include most formally employed urban workers and has indicated its intention to widen the net even further in the future.

How great is the government's future pension liability? In fact, it is among the highest in the world: in present-value terms the government's "implied net pension debt" is estimated to be approximately 80 to 100 percent of GDP, depending on assumptions one makes about the number of persons covered by the pension system, the size of payments to each pensioner (the wage replacement rate), and the worker contribution rate.[8] The size of the eventual future pension debt will also depend on how successful the government is in implementing its plan to transform the pension system from a pay-as-you-go to a funded system.

Given the size of the implied net pension debt, can the government's strong current fiscal position be maintained in the future? That question cannot be answered with confidence, but a number of points are worth noting. First, the government's pension obligations will not become financially unmanageable under current circumstances for another decade or two. Second, even without changing the pension system, there are a number of ways in which this obligation could be met without a fiscal crisis, including raising taxes and diverting expenditures from other uses, issuing debt, or selling state assets. As noted above, tax revenues have been growing rapidly in recent years, and there is still considerable scope in the system to raise them further. Furthermore, the ratio of government debt to GDP, at about 30 percent, is relatively low and, given high GDP growth rates, could be raised, even doubled, without creating severe strains on overall macroeconomic stability. Finally, the government has the potential to raise revenue equal to about 50 percent of GDP by selling off its nonfinancial state-owned enterprises.[9]

The implicit pension debt the government eventually faces will, of course, be less onerous the more successful the government is in making the transition from the current pay-as-you-go system to a funded one, in which workers' contribu-

[8] See, for example, Holzmann, Palacios, and Zviniene 2004; Wang et al. 2000.

[9] According to a UBS study, the book value of China's 150,000 state-owned enterprises is RMB 10 trillion, or about 80 percent of GDP.

tions are held in individual accounts and the government assumes only a partial obligation to fund the pensions of the rapidly growing number of retirees. To induce people to participate in a funded scheme, the financial system must be able to offer a number of attractive long-term saving instruments that yield a reasonably high return, which it currently does not do. This brings us back to the central theme of this study, the imperative of financial sector development for sustaining growth and ensuring stability.

8.7. CONCLUSION

If there were an Olympic event for long-term economic growth, China's performance over the past 25 years would make it a gold medal winner. Perhaps China's economy would have run even faster than it did if reforms had been introduced more rapidly, but that is matter of purely academic interest. What is a more urgent matter is whether rapid growth can be sustained in the future.

China's economy has also been marked by "boom and bust" cycles. Structural changes undertaken since the mid-1990s appear to have moderated the volatility of macroeconomic cycles, but the government still does not have all the tools it needs for the effective conduct of macroeconomic stabilization policy in an economy that is increasingly in the hands of the private sector and operates on market principles.

The main conclusion of this study—that the key to long-term growth and macroeconomic stability is financial sector liberalization and development—is not new or surprising. The financial sector is the last part of the economy to be thoroughly reformed, so it is hardly surprising that the financial sector is the main threat to future growth and stability. It is reassuring that the government is more than aware of this fact and is undertaking to do something about it. The only concern is how urgently or how cautiously the government will proceed. There is a saying that "nothing succeeds like success," which suggests that the government should move as quickly as possible to liberalize and develop the financial system while the economy is still enjoying rapid growth and overall stability. However, it is also the case that often success breeds complacency, a tendency that China must avoid. The Asian financial crisis in 1997–98 demonstrates that in matters of economic growth and stability, fortune-fate-karma can reverse itself surprisingly quickly.

References

Allen, Franklin, Jun Qian, and Meijun Qian. 2005. "Law, Finance, and Economic Growth in China." *Journal of Financial Economics* 77:57–116.

Anderson, Jonathan. 2005a. "China By The Numbers." *Asian Economic Monitor*, UBS Investment Research, May 23, 2.

————. 2005b. "How to Think About China, Part I: State Economy or Market Economy." *Asian Economic Perspectives*, UBS Investment Research, January 6.

————. 2005c. "How to Think About China (Part 2): The Aging China." *Asian Economic Perspectives*, UBS Investment Research, February 7.

————. 2005d. "How to Think about China (Part 3): Which Way Out for the Banking System?" *Asian Economic Perspectives*, UBS Investment Research, May 9.

————. 2005e. "One Gorilla and Four Intellectual Hoops?" *UBS Asian Focus*, March 30.

Aschauer, David Alan. 1989a. "Does Public Capital Crowd Out Private Capital?" *Journal of Monetary Economics* 24:171–88.

————. 1989b. "Is Public Expenditure Productive?" *Journal of Monetary Economics* 23:177–299.

Barnett, Steven. 2004. "Banking Sector Development." In Eswar Prasad, ed., *China's Growth and Integration into the World Economy: Prospects and Challenges*. Washington, DC: International Monetary Fund.

Barth, James R., Rob Koepp, and Zhongfei Zhou. 2004. "Banking Reform in China: Catalyzing the Nation's Financial Future." Unpublished manuscript, February.

Beim, David O., and Charles W. Calomiris. 2001. *Emerging Financial Markets*. Boston: McGraw-Hill/Irwin.

Borensztein, Eduardo, and Jonathan D. Ostry. 1996. "Accounting for China's Growth Performance." *American Economic Review* 86 (2): 224–28.

Bottelier, Pieter. 2004. "China's Emerging Domestic Debt Markets." Working Paper No. 202, Stanford Center for International Development, January.

Boyreau-Debray, Genevieve. Undated. "Financial Intermediation and Growth: Chinese Style." Unpublished manuscript, World Bank.

Cao, Yuanzheng, Yingyi Qian, and Barry Weingast. 1999. "From Federalism, Chinese Style, to Privatization, Chinese Style." Discussion Paper No. 1838, Centre for Economic Policy Research.

Chen, Chien-Hsun, and Hui-Tzu Shih. 2003. "Initial Public Offering and Corporate Governance in China's Transitional Economy." NBER Working Paper No. 9574.

Chen, Yuan. 2003. "Financial System Reform and Economic Development." Speech given at the Seminar on Development and Reform in India and China, New Delhi, November 15.

China Government Securities Depository Trust & Clearing Co. 2003–4. *Monthly Report* (Beijing), various issues.

———. 2004. *Annual Report on China's Securities Market* (Beijing), various issues.

Chow, Gregory C. 1993. "Capital Formation and Economic Growth in China." *Quarterly Journal of Economics* 108 (3): 809–42.

Chow, Gregory C., and Anloh Lin. 2002. "Accounting for Economic Growth in Taiwan and Mainland China: A Comparative Analysis." Unpublished manuscript, Princeton University.

Clarke, George, Lixin Colin Xu, and Heng-fu Zou. 2003. "Finance and Income Inequality: Test of Alternative Theories." World Bank Policy Research Working Paper No. 2984, March.

Clarke, George, Robert Cull, and Maria Soledad Martinez Peria. 2001. "Does Foreign Bank Penetration Reduce Access to Credit in Developing Countries? Evidence from Asking Borrowers." Unpublished manuscript, World Bank Development Research Group, September.

Classens, Stijn, A. Demirguc-Kunt, and Harry Huizinga. 1998. "How Does Foreign Entry Affect the Domestic Banking Market." Unpublished manuscript, World Bank Development Research Group, May.

Classens, Stijn, and Luc Laeven. 2003. "What Drives Bank Competition: Some International Evidence." World Bank Policy Research Working Paper No. 3113, August.

Demirguc-Kunt, A., R. Levine, and H. G. Min. 1998. "Opening to Foreign Banks: Issues of Stability, Efficiency and Growth." In *The Implications of Globalization of World Financial Markets*, Seoul: The Bank of Korea.

Demirguc-Kunt, A., and V. Maksimovic. 1996. "Stock Market Development and Firm Financing Choices." *World Bank Economic Review* 10:341–70.

Demurger, Sylvie. 2001. "Infrastructure Development and Economic Growth: An Explanation for Regional Disparities in China." *Journal of Comparative Economics* 29:95–117.

Demurger, Sylvie, Jeffrey D. Sachs, Wing Thye Woo, Shuming Bao, Gene Chang, and Andrew Mellinger. 2002. "Geography, Economic Policy, and Regional Development in China." NBER Working Paper No. 8897.

Denizer, Cevdet, Raj M. Desai, and Nikolay Gueorguiev. 1998. "The Political Economy of Financial Repression in Transition Economies." Unpublished manuscript.

Eichengreen, Barry. 2003. "China Should Unpeg the Renminbi Now." Unpublished manuscript, August.

Fedelino, Annalisa, and Raju Jan Singh. 2004. "Medium-Term Fiscal Challenges." In Eswar Prasad, ed., *China's Growth and Integration into the World Economy: Prospects and Challenges*. Washington, DC: International Monetary Fund.

Fernald, John, and John H. Rogers. 1998. "Puzzles in the Chinese Stock Market." International Finance Discussion Papers No. 619, Board of Governors of the Federal Reserve System.

Frankel, Jeffrey. 2005. "On the Renminbi: The Choice Between Adjustment Under Fixed Exchange Rate and Adjustment Under a Flexible Rate." NBER Working Paper No. 11274, April.

Fu, Feng-Cheng, Chu-Ping C. Vijverberg, and Wim P. M. Vijverberg. 2004. "Public Infrastructure as a Determinant of Intertemporal and Interregional Productive Performance in China." IZA Discussion Paper No. 1019, February.

Gao, Jian. 1999. *Zhongguo Zhaiquan* [China Securities]. Beijing: jingji kexue chuban she [Economic Sciences Press].

Garcia-Herrero, Alicia, and Daniel Santabarbara. 2004. "Where is the Chinese Banking System Going with the Ongoing Reform?" Occasional Papers No. 0406, Bank of Spain.

Garnaut, Ross, Ligang Song, Yang Yao, and Xiaolu Wang. 2000. *The Emerging Private Enterprise in China*. Canberra: Australian National University Press.

Goldberg, Linda B., Gerard Dages, and Daniel Kinney. 2000. "Foreign and Domestic Bank Participation in Emerging Markets: Lessons from Mexico and Argentina." NBER Working Paper No. 7714, May.

Gordon, Roger H., and Wei Li. 1999. "Government as a Discriminating Monopolist in the Financial Market: The Case of China." NBER Working Paper No. 7110.

Green, Stephen. 2003. *China's Stock Market: Eight Myths and Some Reasons to Be Optimistic.* London: Royal Institute of International Affairs.

Greenwood, Jeremy, and Boyan Jovanovic. 1990. "Financial Development, Growth, and the Distribution of Income." *Journal of Political Economy* 98 (5): 1076–1107.

Gu, Anthony Yanxiang. 2003. "A Trend towards being Normal: The 'A' Share Experience on the Shanghai Stock Exchange." *Applied Financial Economics* 13:379–85.

Guan, Shengyi. 2005. "An Analysis of the Characteristics and Changes in the [Interbank] Bond Market: Jan.–Sept., 2005." Internal publication, CGSDTC (China Government Securities Deposit Trust and Clearing Company).

Gunter, Frank R. 2004. "Capital Flight from China: 1984–2001." *China Economic Review* 14:63–85.

He, Liping, and Xiaohang Fan. 2004. "Foreign Banks in Post-WTO China: An Intermediate Assessment." *China and World Economy* 12 (5): 2–16.

Holzmann, Robert, Robert Palacios, and Asta Zviniene. 2004. "Implicit Pension Debt: Issues, Measurement and Scope in International Perspective." World Bank Social Protection Discussion Paper, March.

Hu, Zuliu F., and Mohsin S. Khan. 1997. "Why is China Growing So Fast?" *International Monetary Fund Staff Papers* 44 (1): 103–31.

Huang, Yasheng. Undated. "FDI, Institutional Biases, and Capital Account Convertibility in China." Unpublished manuscript, MIT Sloan School of Management.

———. 2005. "Why More May Actually Be Less: Financial Bias and Labor-Intensive FDI in China." In Yasheng Huang, Tony Saich, and Edward Steinfeld, eds., *Financial Sector Reform in China.* Harvard University Asia Center, 131–157.

Huang, Yiping. 2002. "Is Meltdown of the Chinese Banks Inevitable?" *China Economic Review* 13:382–87.

Imam, Michael. 2005. "The Chinese Interbank Markets: Cornerstone of Financial Liberalization." *China and World Economy* 12 (5): 17–33.

Jin, Jing. 2003. "Fiscal Federalism or Tax Farming: Political Economy of Fiscal Decentralization in China." Ph.D. diss., Johns Hopkins University.

Jin, Jing, and Hengfu Zou. 2003. "Soft Budget Constraints on Local Government in China." In Jonathan Rodden, Gunnar S. Eskeland, and Jennie Litvack, eds., *Fiscal Decentralization and the Challenge of Hard Budget Constraints*. Cambridge: MIT Press.

Jones, Charles I. 1998. *Introduction to Economic Growth*. New York: W. W. Norton.

Kaminsky, Graciela, and Carmen M. Reinhart. 1999. "The Twin Crises: The Causes of Banking and Balance of Payments Problems." *American Economic Review* 89 (3): (June), 473–500.

Kraay, Aart. 2000. "Household Saving in China." *World Bank Economic Review* 14 (3): 545–70.

Krugman, Paul. 1994. "The Myth of Asia's Miracle." *Foreign Affairs* 73 (December): 62–78.

Kuijs, Louis. 2005. "Investment and Saving in China." World Bank Policy Research Working Paper No. 3633, June.

Kuznets, S. 1974. *Population, Capital, and Growth*. London: Heinemann.

La Porta, Rafael, Florencio Lopez-de-Silanes, Andrei Shleifer, and Robert Vishny. 1998. "Law and Finance." *Journal of Political Economy* 106 (6): 1113–55.

Lardy, Nicholas R. 1999. "The Challenge of Bank Restructuring in China." In *Strengthening the Banking System in China: Issues and Experiences*. Bank for International Settlements Policy Paper No. 7, October.

———. 2002. *Integrating China into the Global Economy*. Washington, DC: Brookings Institution Press.

———. 2003. "Trade Liberalization and Its Role in Chinese Economic Reforms." Unpublished manuscript, Institute for International Economics, Washington, DC.

Lau, L. J., Y. Qian, and G. Roland. 2000. "Reform without Losers: An Interpretation of China's Dual-Track Approach to Transition." *Journal of Political Economy* 108 (1): 120–43.

Laurenceson, James. 2002. "The Impact of Stock Markets on China's Economic Development: Some Preliminary Assessments." Discussion Paper No. 302, University of Queensland.

Lemoine, Francoise. 2000. "FDI and the Opening Up of China's Economy." CEPII Working Paper No. 2000-11, Centre d'études prospectives et d'informations internationales, June.

Levine, Ross. 1998. "The Legal Environment, Banks, and Long-Run Economic Growth." *Journal of Money, Credit, and Banking* 30 (3, pt. 2): 596–613.

———. 2003. "Finance and Growth: Theory, Evidence and Mechanisms." Forthcoming in Philippe Aghion and Steven Durlauf, eds., *Handbook of Economic Growth*. Netherlands: Elsevier Science.

Li, David D. 2001. "Beating the Trap of Financial Repression in China." Unpublished manuscript, Hong Kong University of Science and Technology, March.

Li, Kui-Wai. 1996. "The Productivity of Financial Capital in China's Economic Reform: A Simple Regression Analysis." Unpublished manuscript, City University of Hong Kong.

———. 2003. "China's Capital and Productivity Measurement Using Financial Resources." Yale Economic Growth Center Discussion Paper No. 851, February.

Li, Yang, and Jianfeng Yin. 2005. "Zhongguo de lilu tixi he lilu gaige zhengce: xianzhuangjiqi gaige" [China's Interest Rate System and Interest Rate Policy: Status Quo and Its Reform]. Finance Institute, Chinese Academy of Social Sciences.

Lin, Justin Yifu. 1992. "Rural Reforms and Agricultural Growth in China." *American Economic Review* 82 (1): 34–51.

Lin, Justin Yifu, Fang Cai, and Zhou Li. 2003. *The China Miracle: Development Strategy and Economic Reform*. Rev. ed. Hong Kong: Chinese University Press.

Loayza, Norma, Klaus Schmidt-Hebbel, and Luis Serven. 1998. "What Drives Saving Across the World." Unpublished manuscript, World Bank.

Lu, Susan Feng, and Yang Yao. 2003. "The Effectiveness of the Law, Financial Development, and Economic Growth in an Economy of Financial Depression: Evidence from China." Working Paper No. 179, Center for Research on Economic Development and Policy Reform, Stanford University.

Ma, Guonan, and Ben S. C. Fung. 2002. "China's Asset Management Corporations." Bank for International Settlements Working Paper No. 115, August.

Mankiw, Gregory N., David Romer, and David N. Weil. 1992. "A Contribution to the Empirics of Economic Growth." *Quarterly Journal of Economics* 105 (2): 407–37.

Mei, Jianping, and Jose Scheinkman. 2005. "Speculative Trading and Stock Prices: Evidence from Chinese A-B Share Premia." NBER Working Paper No. 11362.

Modigliani, Franco, and Shi Larry Cao. 2004. "The Chinese Saving Puzzle and the Life Cycle Hypothesis." *Journal of Economic Literature* 42 (March): 145–70.

Naughton, Barry. 1995. *Growing Out of the Plan: Chinese Economic Reform: 1978–1993.* New York: Cambridge University Press.

———. 2002. "Selling Down the State Share: Contested Policy, New Rules." *China Leadership Monitor* 1 (2): 1–10.

Organisation for Economic Co-operation and Development (OECD). 2005. *Economic Survey: China.* Paris: OECD.

Pei, Guifen, and Sayuri Shirai. 2004. "China's Financial Industry and Asset Management Companies: Problems and Challenges." Unpublished manuscript, Keio University, April.

Prasad, Eswar, Kenneth Rogoff, Shang-Jin Wei, and M. Ayhan Kose. 2003. "Effects of Financial Globalization on Developing Countries: Some Empirical Evidence." International Monetary Fund, Occasional Paper No. 220 (September).

Prasad, Eswar, and Shang-Jin Wei. 2005. "The Chinese Approach to Capital Inflows." Unpublished. International Monetary Fund, Research Department, February 20.

Pritchett, Lant. 1996. "Mind Your P's and Q's: The Cost of Public Investment is Not the Value of Public Capital." World Bank Policy Research Working Paper No. 1660, October.

Qi, Zhang, Tao Ran, Liu Mingxing, and Vincent Yiu Por Chen. 2003. "Financial Development and Urban-Rural Income Disparity in China." Presented to the Chinese Economist Society Conference, University of Michigan.

Qian, Yingyi. 1988. "Urban and Rural Household Saving in China." *International Monetary Fund Staff Papers* 35 (4): 592–627.

Qian, Yingyi, and Jinglian Wu. 2000. "China's Transition to a Market Economy: How Far across the River." Unpublished manuscript.

Rawski, Thomas. 1994. "Chinese Industrial Reform: Accomplishments, Prospects, and Implications." *American Economic Review* 84 (2): 271–75.

Riedel, James. 1992. "Public Investment and Growth in Latin America." Unpublished. Inter-American Development Bank, Washington, DC, July.

———. 1993. "Vietnam: On the Trail of the Tigers." *World Economy* 16 (4): 401–22.

———. 2003. "The Tyranny of Numbers or the Tyranny of Methodology: Explaining the East Asian Growth Experience." Unpublished manuscript, Johns Hopkins University.

Ruggles, R., and N. D. Ruggles. 1956. *National Income Accounts and Income Analysis.* 2nd ed. New York: McGraw-Hill.

Sachs, Jeffrey D., and Wing Thye Woo. 1994. "Structural Factors in the Economic Reforms of China, Eastern Europe and the Former Soviet Union." *Economic Policy* 18 (April): 101–45.

———. 2000. "Understanding China's Economic Performance." *Journal of Economic Reform* 4 (1): 1–50.

Scott, Maurice Fitzgerald. 1989. *A New View of Economic Growth.* Oxford: Clarendon Press.

Shirai, Sayuri. 2001. "Banking Sector Reforms in the People's Republic of China: Progress and Constraints." Unpublished. Asian Development Bank.

———. 2002. "Is the Equity Market Really Developed in the People's Republic of China?" Research Paper 41 (September), Asian Development Bank Institute.

———. 2003. "Banks' Performance and Lending Biases in the Case China." Unpublished manuscript, Keio University, March 8.

Shu, Yuan, and Guoqiang Bin. 2002. "The 'Banker Effect' on Chinese Stock Pricing." Paper presented to the International Conference in Honor of Gregory Chow: China and the World Economy, City University of Hong Kong.

Sicular, Terry. 1998. "Capital Flight and Foreign Investment: Two Tales from China and Russia." Unpublished manuscript, University of Western Ontario, January.

Sze, J. W. 1993. "The Allure of B Shares." *China Business Review,* January–February, 817–38.

Usher, D. 1980. *The Measurement of Economic Growth.* Oxford: Basil Blackwell.

Wakabayshi, Masayo, and Landis MacKellar. 1999. "Demographic Trends and Household Saving in China," Interim Report-99-057 (November), International Institute for Applied Systems Analysis.

Wang, Tao. 2004. "China: Sources of Real Exchange Rate Fluctuations." International Monetary Fund Working Paper No. WP/04/18.

Wang, Yan, Dianquing Xu, Zhi Wang, and Fan Zhai. 2001. "Implicit Pension Debt: Transition Cost, Options and Impact of China's Pension Reform." World Bank Policy Research Working Paper, 2555 (February).

Wang, Yan, and Yudong Yao. 2001. "Sources of China's Economic Growth, 1952–99: Incorporating Human Capital Accumulation." World Bank Policy Research Working Paper 2650, July.

Wen, Jaibao. 2005. "Zhong gong zhong yan guan yu zhi ding guo min jing ji he she jhi fa zhan di shi yi ge wunian gui hua de jian yi" [Suggestions by the Party Central Committee on Formulating the Guidelines of the 11th Five-Year Plan for the National Economy and Social Planning], *Xinhua News Agency*, October 19, http://news.xinhuanet.com/politics/2005-10/19/content_2648236_1.htm.

Woo, Wing Thye. 1998. "Chinese Economic Growth: Sources and Prospects." In M. Fouquin and F. Lemoine, eds., *The Chinese Economy*. London: Economica.

———. 1999. "The Real Reasons for China's Growth." *China Quarterly* 41 (January): 115–37.

———. 2001. "Recent Claims of China's Economic Exceptionalism: Reflections Inspired by WTO Accession." *China Economic Review* 12:107–36.

———. 2002. "Some Unorthodox Thoughts on China's Unorthodox Financial Sector." *China Economic Review* 13:388–93.

———. 2003. "The Travails of Current Macroeconomic and Exchange Rate Management in China: The Complications of Switching to a New Growth Engine." Unpublished manuscript, University of California at Davis, November 2.

World Bank. 1995. *China: The Emerging Capital Market*. Report No. 14501-CHA. Washington, DC: World Bank.

———. 2003. *China: Promoting Growth with Equity*. Country Economic Memorandum, October 13.

———. 2004. *China Update*, November.

Wu, Deming. 2004. "Was There Deflation in China Between 1997 and 2002? An Empirical Study of Price Movement in China." Ph.D. diss., Stanford University, June.

Xu, X., and Y. Wang. 1997. "Ownership Structure, Corporate Performance, and Firm's Performance: The Case of Chinese Stock Companies." World Bank Working Paper No. 1794.

———. 1999. "Ownership Structure and Corporate Governance in Chinese Stock Enterprises." *China Economic Review* 10:75–98.

Yang, Dali L. 1997. *Beyond Beijing: Liberalization and the Regions in China*. London: Routledge.

Young, Alwyn. 1995. "The Tyranny of Numbers: Confronting the Statistical Realities of the East Asian Growth Experience." *Quarterly Journal of Economics* 110 (3): 641–80.

———. 2000a. "Gold into Base Metal: Productivity Growth in the People's Republic of China During the Reform Period." NBER Working Paper No. 7856.

———. 2000b. "The Razor's Edge: Distortions and Incremental Reform in the People's Republic of China." NBER Working Paper No. 7828.

Zhang, Jun. 2003. "Zengzhang ziben xincheng yu jisu xuanze: jieshi zhongguo jingji zengzhang xiajiang de yuanyin" [Growth, Capital Accumulation, and Technological Choise: An Explanation for the Long-Run Decline in the Chinese Economic Growth Rate]. In Zhang Jun, ed., *Zhongguo gongye gaige yu jingji zengzhang: wenti yu jieshi* [Industrial Reform and Economic Growth in China: Issues and Explanations]. Shanghai: Shanghai People's Press.

Zhang, Le-Yin. 2004. "The Roles of Corporatization and Stock Market Listing in Reforming China's State Industry." *World Development* 32 (12): 2031–47.

Zhang, Tao, and Heng-fu Zou. 1998. "Fiscal Decentralization, Public Spending and Economic Growth in China." *Journal of Public Economics* 67:221–40.

Zou, Hengfu. 1991. "Socialist Economic Growth and Political Investment Cycles." *European Journal of Political Economy* 7 (1991): 141–57.

Index

Agathon, 2n1
age-dependency ratio, 51
agriculture, 4–6, 38–41
Agriculture Development Bank of China, 105
Allen, Franklin, 78, 82, 86, 89, 90
Anderson, Jonathan, 104–6, 114
A-shares, 135, 136n3, 140
Asian financial crisis, 106, 112, 143–45, 158, 177, 187
Asian Tigers, 23n1
asset management companies (AMCs), 96, 102–4
asymmetric bonds, 83n6

backward specialization, 12
balance-of-payment statistics, 61–62
Bank of China (BOC), 19, 102, 109
banks, 12, 16–17, 66; asset management companies and, 96, 102–4; bond market and, 82–84, 115–16, 119–23, 125–30; break-even condition for, 78n5; capital inadequacy and, 96–98; centralization issues and, 179–81; development strategies and, 90–92; domestic competition and, 106–8; financial flow between sectors and, 45–47; foreign entry and, 109–13; government role and, 94–95; growth and, 85–90; informal finance efficiency and, 89–90; interest rate liberalization and, 77–79, 113–14; key sector features of, 93–95; lending rates and, 99n2; liquidity and, 123–28; loans and, 75–76 (see also loans);

macroeconomic cycles and, 160–61; maturities and, 120–23; Ministry of Finance and, 105, 117–18, 121–23; national income accounting identity and, 45–46; placement and, 118–20; policy banks and, 122–23; privately owned, 75–80, 108–13; problems of, 95–101; profitability and, 98–101; reforms and, 101–14, 160–61; repression of, 70–80; reserve requirements and, 79–80; saving and, 36 (see also saving); state-owned, 75–80, 94–95, 100, 105–9, 121, 127–30, 166–70; stock market and, 135, 139–40; trading and, 123–28
Beim, David O., 71n1, 74
big bang approach, 29
Bin, Guoqiang, 140
bond market, 43, 93, 100, 133; banks and, 82–84, 115–16, 119–23, 125–30; Chinese approach to, 116–18; corporate, 131–32; government bonds and, 118–30; interbank money market and, 123–25, 128–30; Ministry of Finance, 117–18, 121–23; nonperforming loans and, 120; policy banks and, 122–23; role of, 115–16; state-owned commercial banks (SOCBs) and, 119–21, 127, 129–30; STRIPs and, 125; symmetrical bonds and, 125
boom-bust cycles, 4, 114, 186; analysis of, 155–65; investment spending and, 152–55
Borenzstein, Eduardo, 20–21, 26
Bottelier, Pieter, 117